Modernisation: Challenge and Response
(A Study of the Chakpa Community of Manipur)

Modernisation Challenge and Response

(A Study of the Chakpa Community of Manipur)

DR. NINGOMBAM BASANTA

AKANSHA PUBLISHING HOUSE
NEW DELHI-110002 (INDIA)

AKANSHA PUBLISHING HOUSE
4649-B/21, Ansari Road
Darya Ganj, New Delhi - 110 002
Ph.: 23263193 / 9811582579 / 09435116718
Fax: 011-23263193
Email: ektabooks@yahoo.com

Modernisation: Challenge and Response
(A Study of the Chakpa Community of Manipur)

First Published 2008
ISBN 978–81–8370–152–5

[The responsibility for the facts stated, conclusions reached etc., is entirely that of the author. The publisher is not responsible for them, whatsoever.]

PRINTED IN INDIA

Published by Akansha Publishing House, New Delhi and Printed at Aryan Enterprises, Delhi.

CONTENTS

FOREWORD

Andro is an ancient village of the Chakpas, an ancient community of Manipur. Andro has come to Kmean both name of the village and the community living in the village; though actually Andro is the name of the village. But the culture of Andro is a unique culture of Chakpas. There are several Chakpa villages in the Manipur among whom the most prominent are Andro, Sekmai and Phayeng. Dr Ningombam Basanta has made an intensive study on the history, culture, religion and technology of Andro in a UGC sponsored Research Project.

His study aims at the documentation of the present way of life of the Chakpas based on authentic field work. He has utilized manuscripts in dealing with the subject.

Every society is undergoing a change; and each society is in the process of modernization. The Chakpas of Manipur are also under the process of modernization. Dr. Basanta has portrayed the change in the society of Andro.

I hope this work will be well received by the scholars who are interested in the indigenous society and culture of Manipur.

Imphal
7th February, 2008

Gangmumei Kamei

PREFACE

Modernisation: Challenges and Responses: A Study of the Chakpa Community of Manipur. [An improved version of the Project Report submitted to UGC under the title—The Andro-an Eroding Traditional Chakpa Community by the Forces of Modernisation].

The Andros who are an integral part of Meitei community is popular in Manipur for its sense of preserving its age-old customs and traditions. In spite of its sense of preserving things a part of its tradition have faced extinction and many others are also on the way of eroding in their unconscious moments of changes. Interestingly many of the abandoned traditions of the Meities are also flourishing in Andro. However, if the customs and traditions are not properly recorded by writing on paper or by audio-visual means an irreparable damage may happen to such traditions. It is with such intensions that the research is prosecuting so as to disseminate whatever gained from the study to Manipur and outside. So the study is executed in 18 different chapters on various espects of the community i.e., Chapter 1 is introduction which gives a brief account of the community, their migration to 'Nongmaiching' hill and a short account of the hill. Chapter two deals on the traditional mode of settlement including the architecture of a 'Yumjao' and the deities associated with it. Chapter three is on the way of addressing in close relatives and beyond it. Chapter four discusses the birth ceremony *(Yupan Thaba)* and the subsequent ceremonies like *'Yumshengba'* and *'Chak-umba'*. Chapter five gives an account of the different forms of marriage along with marriage rules. It also discusses in brief the practices in-between marriage and child-birth. Chapter six is an attempt on the changes that has taken place in the procedure of disposal of death. It also deals on the beliefs embodied in the practices of death ceremony. Chapter seven is a small compilation of beliefs and practices scattered in everyday life of the community. Chapter eight is also a collection of wits which they practice in their day-to-day life. Chapter nine is a brief discussion on the few socio-cultural institutions of Andro. Chapter ten is a preparation of a calendar of rituals and festivals of Andro which are found prevalent in most of the months of a year. Chapter eleven discusses in brief the two main festivals of Andro, i.e. 'Panam Haraoba' and 'Pureiromba Haraoba'. Chapters twelve and thirteen discuss the power and responsibility of 'Loishang'- the ultimate authority of the village. Chapter fourteen is a selection of a few place names which are possessing a historical or social background in their names. Chapter fifteen is on the existing crafts of Andro but with particular emphasis on pottery. Chapter sixteen is all about the traditional subsistence economy and the likely transformation in the economy in the coming years. Chapter seventeen is a small collection of Chakpa words and sentences which are on record till date and Chapter eighteen is Conclusion.

Dr. Ningombam Basanta

7th February, 2008

ACKNOWLEDGEMENTS

I owe a great deal of thanks to UGC, New Delhi for financial support for this work.

I would like to express my profound thanks to Prof. Gangmumei Kamei for kindly writing the foreword to this book.

I express my sincere thanks to Ph. Achou, Y. Dharmo, Ch. Thambal, Sarubam Ongbi Dharmomala Devi, S. Kulachandra, S. Lalito, S. Thambal, N. Shyam, H. Angousana, Ch. Chandramukta, Ch. Kumar, Ch. Palandro, H. Hemlet Ph. Modon, Ph. Gopal, Ph. (Ongbi) Salam Ningol Chandrabali, Ph. Chandra, Ch. Surchandra, Y. Umachandra-all from Andro, Mutua Bahadur-Director Mutua Masuem.

Author

1

INTRODUCTION

The Chakpas are an integral part of the Meitei community, and they are one of the oldest communities of Manipur. The Chakpas are found mentioned in the manuscript 'Kangbalon'- a royal chronicle containing a chronology of Kings ruled before the Christian era. According to this literature the Chakpas first settled during the reign of King *Moriya Phambalcha*. During his reign the name of this Kingdom was "Tillikoktong Leikoylel Hanna Shemba Konna Loiba Pung-O". *[Its other names were "Meera Pongthoklam Lamthak Sharon Pung-O", and "Muwapalli Leimayon-O", etc.]*. They came with only three lineages namely–"Koikoibam" "Keirambam' and 'Koirekpam. Now the Chakpas settle in the peripheral areas of the valley of Manipur. The Chakpa villages are Sekmai, Koutruk, Pheiyeng, Leimaram, Andro, Kwatha and Khurukhul, etc. The Chakpas settled in the village Andro is also known by the name Andro. Since they constitute one of the earliest settlers of Manipur their culture have been integrated with that of the Meiteis to such a degree that one has become a component of the other. However; the Chakpas, specifically the Andros, still retain their distinctive tradition in spite of their integration with the Meiteis for a period spanning more than two thousand years.

Again the Andros are the tradition bearer of some of the age-old traditions of the Meiteis which the Meiteis have abandoned in due course of time. This peculiar character of preserving the tradition and the very tradition of the Andros have attracted a number of scholars to study this traditional community. In fact the inner strength of the social fabric which handed down their tradition from generation to generation has become a subject which attracts the attention of the scholars. However, a slow transformation that has taken shape in their tradition is also a matter of grave concern. As it happens anywhere in the globe this traditional society also faces the brunt of the mighty force of modernisation. Added to this is also the heavy influence of powerful religions like Hinduism and Christianity. So there arises the need to preserve this age old tradition by all available means before it is too late.

There are oral as well as written accounts of how the Andros came to this village. This village Andro is in the Imphal East District at the eastern foot of Nongmaiching hill which is around 28 km. from Imphal. Their migration history can be traced from manuscripts like 'Sorarel Chakpa Khundarol' and 'Chakpalon Khuntaba' etc. 'Sorarel Chakpa Khundarol' is also known by the name 'Pakhangba Khundoklon.' However, a vivid account of their migration history cannot be produced as there is lake of information both from written and oral accounts.

A. MIGRATION HISTORY

As mentioned earlier in the literature 'Kangbalon' the Chakpas first settled during the reign of king 'Moria Phambalcha'. But a detail account of how the Andros settled in the Nongmaiching hill is available from the literature "Pakhangba Khundoklol". It clearly says that during the reign of King Phambalcha the Chakpas came down from 'Soraren' the Sky. But as this is impossible what is generally accepted is that the Chakpas came from the northerly direction, and they came in two groups - a group of seven known as

"Halleng" and another group of ten known as "Halchok' - whereas the 'Halleng' and 'Halchok' are the name of their progenitors. Chakpane, Tangpane, Pangkakne, Chikchikpane, Laopalne, Sawangne and Sawang Nongphurel Achibane, etc.; they belong to 'Halleng' group. Chakpa, Tangpa; Kashi, Hori, Hora, Nonglol, Nongphu, Melnong Mit, Mellang Mit and Hamengmit belong to "Halchok" group. Further it is mentioned that they arrived at "Mongpa Yoishangkai". However, this is not the name of a place, but this is the name of an office. This is indicative of the presence of a separate department in the palace dealing with the settlement issues. It also reflects a manner of reporting first to the administration by a group of new settlers in the valley and subsequently the authority concerned allots a tentative area for their settlement. And such an arrangement is reflective of the strategic areas settled by the Chakpas in the periphery of the valley. As for instance the Andros in the eastern frontier of the valley was to face the tribes in the east particularly the 'Luhoopas', the Sekmais in the north was to face the Paomai, Mao, Maram, etc., Leimaram, Phayeng, Khurukhul, etc. were to face the Kabuis or any intruder from the west. They were to face any external aggression first before it was relayed to the palace. In addition to this they were also assigned to produce a specific item for use particularly in the palace. For example, the Andros produced pottery items and the Fayeng produced silk clothes. On their departure from the office they cooked food at 'Nongmeipung', a place located at a walking distance from 'Kangla', the traditional temporal seat of Manipur. Both the groups cooked small fry fish, but of unequal items. 'Halleng' group cooked 'Ngakha' fish and 'Halchok' group cooked 'Ngaching' fish (prawn). Again, here, this is also suggestive of accompanying fishing implements in their migration. In no time 'Halleng' finished their cook and prepared for their destination. But 'Halchok' could not do so and they took much time. Simple reason was that 'Ngaching' (prawn) becomes red when it is cooked. They considered that the food was not well cooked and was not fit for eating. So they boiled it further till the fish becomes white. *It seems the Chakpas were not familiar with the small fish 'Ngaching'. They were not aware of the nature of the fish.* 'Halleng' group could not wait 'Halchok' group. They suggested to proceed in advance before the sun sets so as to find out their place of settlement. So the 'Halleng' group advised the 'Halchok' group to follow their footprint. So they left 'Nongmeipung' by leaving marks by swords on a tree named 'Lammuk'. Finally they settled at a place named 'Mangshi'.

'Nongmeipung' mound–near this mound 'Halleng' and 'Halchok cooked their food.

Meanwhile the 'Halchok' group boiled the food till it becomes white. But they failed and they wrongly realised that the food was poisoned and not proper to consume. So they wrapped the cooked food by seven leaves of 'Khangla' tree. 'Khangla' leaf is used in many rites and rituals of the Andros. *They also use to wrap the 'Naopham'* (placenta or umbilical cord) by *"Khangla' leaves and bury it nearby the house as a tradition.* A small mound was made nearby the buried food and since then the mound came to be known as "Khangla Pung". *This 'KhangJapung' is around six hundred feet to the north of 'Nongmeipung'. At present their is no remain of 'Khanglapung', however, a probable site can be located as the place named 'Soibam Leikai' Khanglapung is derived from the mound 'Khanglapung'.*

As for information there is another mound named'Lamdaipung' just near at the north of 'Nongmeipung'. So *'Lamdaipung' is in between Nongmeipung and 'Khanglapung'. As a result Khanglapung' is little farther away from Lamdaipung. The presence of these 'Pungs' and more other Pungs (mounds) in Manipur says that there was mound culture in the region. Mounds might have been prepared to tell something to the posterity about an event of national or historical importance. At present there are many means and devices to relay such tells to posterity. However, in those days the only easy means was to prepare such* a *mound which would withstood from the wear and tear of wind, rain, water and from foreign invasion. Again in the valley there are not suitable huge stones to erect monoliths, so the only means was to prepare mounds.* So *there are many Pungs like 'Nongmeipung', 'Lalampung', Charoipung', Thijitpung, Shingjupung, 'Kakwa Lamtaipung', Kongba Soudongpung, 'Khuraipung', 'Wangthonbipung', etc.* Without any thing to eat 'Halchok' group soon followed the 'Halleng' group with great hunger. But the attempt bore no fruit. They followed the marks left on trees. Unfortunately the tree was 'Lammuk' a tree which the bark becomes dark as soon as it is cut. They concluded that the mark was an old one and it could not be a new route. So they remained confused and could not proceed further. And returned to a suitable place. In traditional parlance the one who departed is known as 'Yangoiba'. And the one who stays is known as 'Teroure', 'Haldro'. In due course of time 'Haldro' was corrupted into the present 'Andro'. It settled on 'Nongmaiching'. hill. The sentence *"Langmaichingta Khul Takhiye"* clearly shows that the Andros first settled on the Nongmaiching hill. Now a days they are settled at the foot of the hill spreading around three km. in length from the southern edge (Khunou Leikai) of the village to the northern edge (Machengpat Leikai) of the village. As found from archaic literatures like 'Pakhangba Khundoklol', etc. 'Khunungmayum' is the lineage of 'Halchok'. Now this is transformed into 'Khunnumayum'. This lineage is found involved in many major rituals of the village. It may be a way of extending due respect to the lineage considering its old age. Now a days there are around sixteen lineages in Andro. Another important lineage is 'Ningthoujam'.

The migration history of the Andros, to be more specific the Chakpas, is still a controversy. At one time, it is widely believed that they settled at Koubru range (a range in the north-western side of the valley. However, according to literature "Leishemlon' the 'Lai' tribe first settled in the 'Koubru' range. It is clearly mentioned in the literature describing the range in the manner ... *"Awang Koubru Ashuppa, Laiyam Khunda Ahanba ..."* etc. which says Awang Koubru the supreme authority, a place first settled by the 'Lais'. It was from this range that they spread to other hills surrounding the valley. In other literatures like 'Poireiton Khunthokpa', 'Ningthourol Lambuba' 'Moirang Ningthourol Lambuba', etc. the Chakpas has been in existence since the early time.

Mindomin Taung (Princess of hill) is found mentioned as Angooching or Chakpa Angooching (Hill of Chakpa Angoo) in the literature 'Ningthourol Lambuba'. This 'Angooching' (Angoo hill) is a range running north to south of the Kabow valley (now in Burma, at one time the territory of Manipur, ceded to Burma first in A.D. 1834 by the British and secondly in A.D. 1953 by India). Chindwin river in this valley is known to the Meiteis as Ningthee or Chakpa Ningthee. And according to the literature 'Ningthourol Lambuba' Ningthee (Engthee) is a Chakpa (Thet) word. In an article by 'Maw Nwee Than' in the magazine 'Kabow Valley' it is found mentioned that the first known settler of this valley was Tet or thet or sak at about 900 B.C. These Thet peoples (Chakpa) spread from Manipur and settled in this valley. Before their settlement some unknown tribes were there (probably the Lai or Zo tribe). The article continues that due to repeated raid by the otiginal inhabitants the Thet or Tet (Chakpa) shifted to the Irrawady valley and some of them might have shifted back to Manipur.

This view of migration of Chakpas from Kabow Valley to Manipur Valley is corroborated by local beliefs. The belief associates with their principal deity 'Panam'. During 'Panam Haraoba' festival it is believed that the deity appears in the sky in the depth of night beginning from south-eastern direction and vanishes in the community forest of the village in the form of a ball of fire. The direction implies the direction of Kabow Valley.

The controversy over the migration of the Chakpas will exist till on all out effort is made to trace the migration of other groups constituting the Meitei community. However, it is certain that the Andros to be more exact, the Chakpas migrated to Manipur in the beginning of history of Manipur. After their departure from 'Nongmeipung' the Andros first settled on the eastern side of 'Nongmaiching' hill. The sentence *'Langmaichingta Khul Takhiye'* from the literature 'Sorarel Chakpa Khundarol' clearly says that the Andros settled in the Nongmiching hill. It says that they established a village in the 'Nongmaiching'. However, they were not alone in the Nongmaiching hill. The Shelloi-Langmais ruled the 'Nongmaiching' hill. The Shelloi-Langmais later on merged to Angom Salai (clan). Again there were villages like Haokap Chingsang, Ngangching, Khulpham, Thanga

Youkham, etc. Besides there were Tangkhul (tribe) villages in the Nongmaiching hill. 'Huitok' and 'Sharam' are the two Tangkhul villages found mentioned in 'Panthoipi Khongkul'.

It is certain that the Andros once settled in the hills. However, it remains a question that when the Andros came down from the hill to settle on the foothill. The literature 'Chakpalon Khuntaba' says that during the reign of King Naokhamba (A.D. 411-428) there were ten Chakpa villages in 'Nongmaiching' hill. But during the reign of King Punshiba (A.D. 1404-1432) the Andros were well established in the foothill. There are still remains of their settlement in the hills. Artifacts like pots (pieces) or pottery items are found at the site of the settlement. Iron implements in pieces are also found there. According to Yumkhaibam Dharmo Singh, former 'Khullakpa' (Village Chief) of Andro Awang Leikai, at least two places namely 'Salang'; and 'Ayang' with clear evidence of settlement of villages is available at present. It is on near plane slop of the hill. And it is a place which can accommodate a number of houses. Water streams which were once used by the settlers are also available there.

The water streams, the near plane slopes, the remains of pottery items, and tools and implements are the hard reminders of the then settlement. There is a place named 'Changathen' which is now transformed into 'Changaithembi' - a place for pilgrimage. But there is a background on the name of this particular place. 'Uchon' is a village sandwicked by bigger villages namely 'Huikap' and Andro. Near this village 'Uchon' there is an open field. This open field was once the paddy field of 'Ayang' village in the hill which is more than 3 km from the village. There is also another place named 'Nongmairou'. And this was the field for the village 'Sakuba'. In the version of Y. Dharmo Singh even during his lifetime there was a practice of carrying 'Chakyom' (packaged food) in the workplace or on the way to workplace by the female members of the family. As the field or workplace was far away from home so it was inconvenient for someone to proceed to home for his meal. There was also the factor for time. So in order to save time and as well as to reduce the hardship of hunger it was a practice to wait the man on the field with his 'Chakyom' (packaged food) at the place named 'Changthen'. From this practice of waiting the villagers with 'Chakyoms' who went for work in the paddy field then the place came to be known as 'Changathen'.

But in due course of time it was transformed into 'Chakngaithembi'. But now it is deified and has taken the shape of a deity. And every year on the third day of 'Kalen' (May) the villagers of Andro visit the place as a pilgrim and perform rite at the spot. However, the transformation was such that from 'Chakngaithen' to 'Changathen' and finally to 'Changaithembi'. 'Chakngaithen' literally means a place for waiting one's meal. Chak=rice=meal, Ngai=Ngaiba=to wait, Then=a plane area in the hill. Around this 'Changathembi' there is a stream named 'Thoubom Houbi'. 'Thoubom' is a tall flowering grass. This tall flowering grass 'Thoubom' grows around this stream and hence the name 'Thoubom Houbi'.

After settling on the 'Nongmaiching' hill for a considerable period of time the Andros descended from the hill and settled near the foot of the hill. The way how they descended from the hill and the year when that was effected is still a question which remain unanswered. Naturally shifting villages from hill to valley takes many years as it is dangerous to shift at a time as children cannot tolerate the changed environment. And simply the children dies.

For Andro 'Khuman Leikai' is considered the first place of settlement and treated as the oldest 'Leikai' (local). But today there are as many as 14 Leikais with a population above five thousands. The Leikais (locals) are 1. Khuman Leikai, 2. Makha Leikai, 3. Awang Leikai, 4. Mamang Leikai,

5. Kharam Leikai. *In this Leikai there is a small population of Kharam tribe and hence the name of the 'Leikai' as "Kharam Leikai'. The life-style and physical appearance of the 'Kharams' are almost identical with the Andros. Unless someone guides one will consider the Kharams* as *Andros.* 6. Khunou Leikai, 7. Chinggol Leikai, 8. Machengba Leikai, 9. Loupaochum Leikai, 10. Erao Ching Leikai, 11. Nungyungbi Leikai, 12. Leitianpekpham Leikai, 13. Champra Leikai and 14. Sanapat Leikai. There are fifteen lineages and they are Meitei lineages which are as follows: 1. Yumkhaibam, 2. Heikrujam, 3. Leishungbam, 4. Phanjoubam, 5. Sagolshem, 6. Ningthoujam. 7. Shamchetshabam, 8. Puthem, 9. Thokchom. 10. Chingakham, 11. Hijam, 12. Salam, 13 Asheibam, 14. Sarubam, and 15. Sarungbam. For the Meiteis there are seven Yeks (exogamous clans), however, for the Andros there are only six Yeks. And they are 1. Khuman, 2. Ningthouja, 3. Moirang, 4. Kha-Nganba, 5. Luwang and 6. Angom.

B. TOPOGRAPHY

Almost on all sides of the village there are rice fields. A stream known as 'Ahong Turel' passes in the heart of the village. It runs on the eastern edge of 'Pureiromba' deity (or shrine). The direction of the stream is west to east. Now the stream comes out of the village running near the public crematorium and meets with 'Nongmai Turel', a much bigger stream. The name 'Ahong,' may be derived from a place named 'Ahongkei' - a place with a huge stone at the lower part of the hill (Nongmaiching). It is a sacred place for the Andros. This stream 'Ahong' originates from this side of the hill where there is a huge stone. So the name of the stream as 'Ahong- Turel'. The 'Nongmai Turel' runs north to south at the eastern edge of the paddy field adjoining the eastern range. A bridge on this stream connects 'Sanapat Leikai' with the rest of the village. The river on the southern side of the bridge is known as 'Erang turel' and that of the northern side is known as 'Nongmai Turel'. In the eastern side of the village there are lakes namely (1) Poirou Pat, (2) Sanapat and (3) Laipat. Some ten years back parts of the lakes were covered with lotuses and lilies. Now this is completely removed and converted into paddy fields.

There are places like 'Leitanpekpham' and 'Champra Chingdong'. They are places for collecting raw materials for pottery. From 'Leitanpekpham' they extract clay. Again the other component 'Leichreng', they extract it from 'Champrachingdong'- a small hillock in the village. Again there is the 'Kekopat'- a small pond where the water is used in cooking in 'Panam Haraoba' festival. There are other places like 'Amamlok'. 'Changathen' and 'Waktrong'. They are sacred places.

Again 'Lamphal Shoi' and Uran Lakpa' are the extremities of the village. 'Lamphel Shoi' in the east and Uran Lakpa' in the west. Every year on the day of 'Lam Haiba'- a ritual marking the arrival of dry season, offerings are paid to deities which are considered as sentinels of the village at this two places. On the northern side of the village there is a reserved forest, reserved for the deity 'Panam'. However, for daily offering a secluded place is maintained in the village with 'Panam Laipu' as the person in charge of the deity 'Panam'. Andro society is basically a patriarchal society. However, the Maibis, the priestesses are given due share in their engagements relating to rituals. So there are secluded places in the outskirts of the village: The three places are 'Maibi Phampham' at 'Sanapat'; one at the reserve forest of Panam and the other at 'Santhong'- the place where the ritual 'Kurak Lamtaiba' is observed. But the one which attracts visitors in the village is the temple for 'Androgi Mei'- the Andro fire at the heart of the village. Formerly the fire was housed in a small hut. Now it is transformed into a big temple.

This fire is believed to be handed over by the legendary coloniser–the 'Poireiton' of the first century A.D. Utmost care is taiken not to occur any break in the fire. And it has established as a socio-cultural institution. However, it is not free from controversy. Because 'Poireiton' himself came across the Andros using fire in cremation. The following para from the archaic literature 'Poireiton Khunthok' is a testimony on how fire was familiar with the Andros for their use in many utility services. And he excerpt runs as follows - *Yiyuwa Chingkhong Poireitonna Yotpi Cheishu Mathoukumna Nongpok Tampu Kenna Shenpi Shidaba Kabow Natapapu Leirikpara Haina khunthirakpapu Chakpa Kaitong Hao Pahangpa Shing Chang Lengta Thongpa Pamel Tangkhai Laopata Paohangkhiye. Chakpa keitong Pakhangpa-O, Meipu Takhongi Pai, Meikhu Nonglol Kapa Ashipu Kari Meino Paohangpapu Hempa Puchet Mei, Chekai Kakup Mei, Charu Tangshoi Mei, Loimom Poktok Mei, Phutit Nonglol Meira Haina Paohang Papu Hoita Yiyuwa Chingkhong Poireiton* O *Aiyum Hemcheng Fuyikumei, Charu Tangshoi Meishung, Nate .... Meerou Meine Haina Paokhumkhiye'.* A *version in modern Manipuri runs thus - 'Eyuwa Chingkhong Poireitonna Yotki Cheishu Tumba Makhei Nongpok Maikeigi Tampak Pumnamakta Kabo Shida Nadaba Karamba Khul Leiramgadabage Haina Thirakpada Chakpa Keitongba Hao Pakhang, Shingchang Marengbanda Thongduna Chatpa. U Tangkhai Khaiba Amada Wa Hangkhi, Keitongba Chakpa Pakhangba-O, Mei Chakpagi Tang-goi Paiduna Meikhu Wangna Kariba Ashibu Karigi Meino ? Haona Pam Thaba Meira, Chaphu Ekpa Meira, Charukhok Thaba Meira, Fou Pokpa Meira, Charu Fudit Thabagi Meira Haina Hangbada Chakpa Pakhangna Hairak-e, Hoi Eyuwa Chingkhog Poireiton-O, Eikhoi Chakpagi Chaphu Ekpagi Mei, Charukhok Thabagi Meishu Natte. Chakpa Potloi Meine. Leima Falloung Ngambeegi Machanipa Shangphuraipa Koubado Kharadagi Onthaduna Shire. Eikhoi ChakpagiMee Thabagi Mei, Mee Potloibagi Meini Haina Khumkhi.* It says Poireiton, in his mission to find out a habitable place in the eastern side of the valley with his iron staff, came across a Chakpa youth with an axe on his shoulder. On seeing a blazing fire he enquired the reason for the fire. Is the fire meant for slash and burn, for igniting pot in pottery, for burning straws in the field or for puffing rice? Non of the activities was related with the fire, replied the Chakpa youth. The fire was meant for cremation. A boy named 'Shangphuraipa', the son of 'Leima Phalloungambi' was drowned in the pond. The fire was meant for burning man, for cremation, said the youth (Chakpa).

From the above statement what is revealed is that the Andros were familiar with fire and fire was used for many purposes ranging from pottery to puffing rice. So the belief that the Andro fire was introduced by 'Poireiton' contradicts with the above statement where the Andros had the knowledge to use fire for many utility services.

But here one cannot dilute the belief on finding the facts from literature. 'The belief might have its socio-economic and cultural background. Because Poireiton is such a person who accompanied with a civilization in his mission to find out a habitable place in the region. The mission was executed with the knowledge of different aspects of life relating to food items including a variety of vegetables, weaving implements, artisans for jewellery, a variety of paddy including the famous "Chahou-Poireiton"- the black rice and blacksmith, etc. In other sense the arrival of 'Poireiton' helped in the development and transformation of life. So it is not an awkward attitude to develop an aura of myth around such a person. It may be treated as a sense of extending due reverence to such a personality who has transformed the life so much. It is not wrong to remember such a person in the form of preserving the fire.

C. SOCIO-CULTURAL SITUATION

There cannot be an independent economy of Andro and it is an appendage of Manipur economy. Agriculture is still the mainstay of the economy with the right to individual ownership. However, in some specific items communal ownership is also still prevalent. But what is emerging is the small group of employees in the state and central government services.

Formerly 'Loishang' the village administrative body was the supreme authority in civil and judicial matters. With the replacement of monarchy by democracy in Manipur a certain portion of its power has been shared to the State. Now 'Loishang is reduced to a body looking after the rites and rituals of the village. However, it still exercise its power on disputes of the nature of marriage, thefts etc. But if the case becomes complex the right is given to a person to appeal to a court of the State.

Most of the rituals and festivals are similar with that of the Meiteis. Again there are rituals which are purely for the Andros and not available in Meitei tradition. The ritual 'Lam Haiba' is not found among the Meiteis. Again in the rituals and festivals which are similar in names with that of the Meiteis, there we find a number of differences ranging from procedure, timing, items offered and the deity prayed, etc.

Pottery is an old craft of the Andros and they are the one who supplied earthen wares to the kings of Manipur. As pottery is a major plank of their economy, so due importance is given to it in the form of certain codes in extracting the raw materials. In addition rites are performed every year marking the day of beginning the extraction of raw materials. But still pottery is at the traditional level and introduction of advance technology is necessary. Fishing and weaving implements, though traditional, is still supporting their economy. Certain modernisation is found in wood work, however bamboo work is still traditional and has its place in Andro Society. Fishing implements and musical tools are also still traditional. However, in agriculture modernisation has arrived as far as ploughing is concerned.

The Andro dialect is still there at least in record with nowhere its place for use except at the time of certain rituals. There are names of seven days and twelve months. Also there are the names of heavenly bodies, birds, cattle, foods and vegetables, etc. And certain sentences can also be produced out of the vocabulary.

Some of the socio-cultural institutions are still flourishing while a few are slowly succumbing to the forces of modernisation. Organisations like 'Pujari Loishang' and 'Arangpham Loishang' are still popular. However, 'Shinnaipham Kaba', the only institution for the girls is gradually disappearing from the village. It survives only at the interior areas of the village. The ritual named 'Maibi Chaklon Katpa' - a ritual performed as a token for the festivals 'Panam Haraoba' and 'Pureiromba Haraoba' when both are failed to perform in the village, is becoming a regular practice since the pass few years. And this will continue to do so, as the village cannot held the 'Haraoba' festivals. This ritual is by far a ritual for the Maibis (priestess) where due liberty is granted to them as regard to their behaviour, actions and responsibilities. However, as regard freedom to women (in a patriarchal society) of Andro it is next to the ceremony 'Epan Thaba' (birth ceremony) where one can witness an all women affair.

D. ACCOUNT OF NONGMAICHING HILL

The study may be incomplete if an account of 'Nongmaiching hill' is not included in the research. It was once on the hill where the Andros settled for a pretty long time. In this age also they are not far away from the hill but have climbed down at the foot. The hill is the source of their material culture. It provides water for irrigation and drinking purposes. The forest at the foothill shelters the secluded place of their principal deity 'Panam'. The two varieties of soil, one' Leichreng' (coarse soil) and the other 'Leitan' (clay), both on the different heights of the hill, is the source of their art of pottery. Woods, bamboos and thatch grown in the hill have influenced in moulding the architecture of their house. In brief the hill directly or indirectly influences in developing their culture and tradition.

A view of 'Nongmaiching' hill from the East

Physical Feature

The 'Nongmaiching' hill is around 5133 ft, above the sea level. The literature 'Panthoibi Khongkul' gives an account of the hill including its physical feature, climate and natural vegetation, etc. The hill is composed of nine (9) ranges with nine (9) faces which says *'Chingsha Mapal Shuna Leiba Ching, Chingmaishu Mapal Shuna Panba Ching'*. It has seven (7) gorges and like the rooms of a house it has three stages which says.' *Loktaretna Chenthaba Ching, Yumgi Kagumna Fidup Ahum Shuba Ching'*. There are hot places and cold regions in the hill. It is a hill which experiences scattered snowfall. It also says that it was surrounded by water and further mention that water is a constituent of the hill. It gives us the idea that it produces a lot of water, may be due to its lust forest. Even some thirty (30) years back one could hear the sound of gushing water down the hill during rainy season from a distance of around five (5) kms. which is popularly known as 'Nongmaiching Eraokhol'. Further, it is described as a majestic hill, a hill created at the foremost during the creation of the world - a piece from the Meitei Creation theory which says that - the hills were pulled up by the Almighty from primeval water in the course of creation of the world. As fixed by nails of iron and gold the hill is not shaken by earthqu'ake. It continues that there are iron and gold ores. The hill was made by the sword named 'Shamba' .

The mode of cultivation by that time was slash and burn. And rain was the only source of irrigation. At least double crops were cultivated early crop (Angal Phou) and later crop. Besides rice other vegetables like arum, ginger, cha-en (bajra) etc, were also cultivated. Spade was the dominant agricultural tool which was used in spadework, uprooting the herbs and shrubs and putting the soil upside down, etc. At least two early paddy; 'Cha-el' and 'Thang-e' were cultivated in the hill. Foukak, Haocheng, Khollol and Paomel, etc, were the varieties cultivated during the rainy season.

Nongmaiching hill is closely related with culture of the Meiteis as evidenced by the literature' Shakok Thiren' and 'Leihou Nonghou Puya'. The literature deals with the background of the name of the hill 'Nongmaiching'. In addition it also furnishes the circumstances leading to the birth of seven days of a week. The story begins with a myth, however, there are elements of migration history, migrating from 'Koubru' hill to 'Nongmaiching' hill. It also reveals the ecology of the then period. It says, in the past the valley was covered by a sheet of water. " Epuroi Apokpa", the supreme deity contemplated to convert the valley in the model of heaven. So he advised 'Lainingthou Sorarel' to translate his ambition into reality, 'Epuroi Apokpa' pointed to the mighty hill standing in the east of 'Koubru and ordained him to level the hill to the ground so as to fill the valley with the soil (earth) from the hill. 'Lainingthou Sorarel was blessed by 'Epuroi Apokpa' to rule both the heaven and earth. Encouraged by the blessing 'Lainingthou Sorarel' in association with 'Laiyams' (deities) constructed a huge boat called' Heiyang Hirel' from the tree named 'Uyaini' which are available in 'Koubru' hill. 'Koubru' hill is situated on the north-western side of the Imphal valley, and this hill is much taller than 'Nongmaiching' hill. The 'Laiyams' crossed the sheet of water on the boat like a dragon wades in the water.

They arrived at the foot of 'Nongmaiching', and 'Lainingthou Sorarel' was amazed by the majestic height of the hill which was found touching the clouds. The place where they anchored the boat was named as 'Hiyangthang', Considering the height of the hill which touches the 'Nong' (cloud) it was named as 'Nongmaiching'. They scaled the hill led by the king of 'Laiyam' and the day was named as 'Ningthoukaba' where 'Ningthou' is king and 'Kaba' is to climb. After scaling the hill the 'Lais' standing at the top of it labelled the hill by using thunderbolt. And the day was named as 'Leipakpokpa' where 'Leipak' is earth 'or soil and 'Pokpa' is to give birth. And thus a labelled ground was given on the day and hence the name 'Leipakpokpa'. After acquiring a suitable land the 'Lais' erected their house. Such a day was named as 'Yumshakeisha' where 'Yum' is house. The early settlers on the hill were Hao's, a tribe. On seeing the activities of the 'Lais' the 'Haos' attacked the 'Lais'. And a fierce battle was fought on elephant and horseback. The day was marked as 'Shagolshen' where 'Shagol' is horse. As a result of the terrible fight between 'Lais' and 'Haos' the field became red with blood. From such a scene the name 'Erai' was coined. The day when the blood stained weapons like sword, spear, arrow, etc.of both the sides were washed was known as 'Thangja' where' Thang' is sword. So when an account is given on ' Nongmaiching' hill it is described as a hill which produces the seven (7) days of a week. The seven days in order are 1. Nongmaiching (Sunday), 2. Ningthoukaba (Monday), 3. Leipakpokpa (Tuesday), 4. Yumshakeisha (Wednesday). 5. Shagolshen (Thursday), 6. Erai (Friday), 7. Thangja (Saturday).

The cultural and historical significance of the hill is described poetically in the following manner:

Nongmaigidi Haitha Ching,
Nongpok Khanlong Mapungyai,
Panthoibi Emana Konba Lam,
Nonggi Mammai Faona Wangba Ching
Taibang Chayom Taret Thokna-ching
Nongmai Hagabara Hada ching
Seroi Mana Nik-Kabara Nikta ching
Loibi Chinqmai Mapal Fangba Chingjaoni,.

The 'Nongmaiching' hill is a great geographical barrier for the Andros. The hill keeps them geographically isolated from the mainland Meitei society, particulprly from the population of Imphal, the capital of Manipur. The hill also served as a mental barrier which tended to develop a psychology of their own. They still suffer from a complex, and consider themselves as inferior. And they still feel the sense of being exploited by the Meiteis, a legacy of Hindu feudalism which the Manipuris suffered as a whole. However, they still publicly claim that they still retain their culture and tradition. And here arises the big question mark of how long will they be able to retain their culture and tradition. But the reality is that certain amount of their custom and tradition has been eroded which are manifested in their unconscious moments of cultural and traditional activities.

Most of their traditional personal names like Achou, Tompok, Maipak, etc,. have been replaced by Surchandra, Dharmo, Palandro, etc. And this prevails in other areas of custom and tradition. The study gives the opportunity to record their custom and tradition side by side to fathom the amount of erosion that had occured in their tradition and culture.

REFERENCES

1. Kangbalon – MS
2. Sorarel Chakpa Khundarol MS
3. Chakpalon Khuntaba – MS
4. Pakhangba Khundoklon – MS
5. Poireiton Khunthokpa – MS
6. Ningthourol Lambuba – MS
7. Moirang Ningthourol Lambuba – MS
8. Panthoipi Khongkul – MS
9. Nongmaiching Chingoiron – MS
10. Naothingkhong Phambal Kaba – MS
11. Shelloi Langmailon – MS
12. Shakok Thiren – MS
13. Leihou Nonghou Puya. – MS

.1. Oral interview with Pdt. Moirangthem Noren.
2. Oral interview with Ph. Achou, Andro Mamang Leikai.
3. Oral interview with Ph. Y. Dharmo Singh, former Khullakpa.
4. A seminar paper presented by Dr. L. Suresh.
Title: Chin the Khyang Ethnic group.

2

TRADITIONAL HOUSE AND HOUSEHOLD DEITIES

TRADITIONAL MODE OF SETTLEMENT

In the past this valley of 2238sq.km. was not a place as it is now. Marshy lands and lakes were abundant where the biggest was Loktak lake. So, the habitable areas might not be plenty as it is now. In such a situation the mode of settlement was quite different from to-day's. Such a mode of settlement might have been influenced primarily by the strategic location of the valley and its demographic situation. Whatever might be the influence the fact is that a homestead was as big as three paris, sometimes four paris of land where a 'Pari' is equal to around 2.5 acres. And these homesteads were arranged successively till the last habitable areas. The vestiges of such homestead is still found in the heart of Imphal. Such vestiges are in existence in great numbers in rural areas. Some of them are abandoned homesteads and are converted into paddy fields. But still the boundary of such a homestead is entact.

A part of such homestead was utilised for rice cultivation. But the remaining was meant for the cultivation of different varieties of vegetables beans and pulses. A number of beans; peas, chouhawai, hawai ashangbi, koli hawai, vegetables; cabbage, mustard plants gourd, sebot, yendem, chilli, ginger, turmeric, banana plants and potato, etc., were planted in the homestead. Silk worm was reared. Cane sugar was planted. Besides there was a place for thatch garden. However, cotton plantation was not so much popular. The required cotton was got from the hills. The dissolution of such homesteads began after the World War-II. Since then such a homestead became the home of many families. And families began clubbing together in urban and rural areas of Imphal valley. Such a mode of settlement has become a thing of the past in the urban areas of Imphal.

MAINTENANCE OF HOMESTEADS

It was in this big homestead that a Yumjao stood magnificently at one time. In most of the cases these homesteads were rectangular in shape. A ditch is dug around the homestead. And the earth so collected from the ditch makes a raised earthen wall called 'Leipan' in the inner side of the homestead. The ditch served to drain water from the garden as well as an obstacle to an intruder or to cattle. In strategic areas of the wall spikes made of bamboo or the like is strucked so as to act as weapon preventing the cattle or the intruder from entering the garden. It is known as "Shou-Thakpa". It was on this 'Leipan' that bamboo was planted. But bamboo is planted mostly in the western and northern wall of the homestead. In those areas of the Leipan where bamboo was not grown fencing was erected.

The Hojang or Konthong (gate) was made in the Chingkhei (northeast) of the Yumjao. A pond was dug in the eastern part of the garden near the eastern wall. The earth so collected from the pond was placed on the eastern wall (Leipan) making the earthen wall nearby the pond making little higher than the rest of the Leipan. This raised portion would hide the house and the activities in the courtyard to a new corner. The area in between the pond and the gate was another place for banana plantation. Banana was planted in the north western area near the western wall of the garden also. The area at the back of the Yumjao was served for piggery. The Amangsang (lavatory) was located at the south-western side of the house. Banana was not planted in the southern side of the house because it was considered inauspicious which would bring bad fortune to the family.

YUMJAO AND OUT-HOUSES

A yumjao of five or four rooms stood in the homestead mostly at the backside of the garden leaving more space in the eastern side of the garden. This Yumjao was surrounded by many out houses of different uses. The back door was placed at the last room which also served as kitchen. The back door was opened at the left wall of the last room. So, the place around the back door was served as 'Lukhak Kom' (garbage).

The left and right sides of the house around the middle of the house was used in making nest for chicken. Awang Sangoi (at the northern side of the courtyard), Makha Sangoi (at the southern side of the courtyard), Mamang Sang-goi (at the eastern side of the courtyard). Shang-gon, Chabokshang, Ya-ongshang, Foukei, Singkei, etc., were the out-houses. Awang Sang-goi and Makha Sang-goi were mostly decoration of the house. And they were used occasionally at family functions like marriage, death ceremony, birth ceremony, ear-piercing ceremony etc. The Mamang Sang-goi was bigger in size and it served a number of purposes. The southern side of it was the place for rice pounding. The loom was placed in the eastern side of it. The loin loom was fixed on the northern wall of the Mamang Sang-goi The open space between the Yumjao and the Mamang Sang-goi was the Shumang (courtyard). In the centre of the courtyard a shrub (either Tairen or Tulsi) was planted. The circular place around the plant in the courtyard was the 'Thelong' a neat place which is cleaned by scrubbing with a 'Nura' (traditional brush) with water everyday. This 'Thelong' is the place where anything to be distributed to persons present in a ceremony was placed. It is also the place for performing rituals of certain ceremonies like "Na Hutpa" (ear-piercing). "Polangkhok" (a pole for hanging cloths) was placed in the northern side of the courtyard near the Awang Sang-goi. It was not placed at the right side of the courtyard.

The Shang-gon (cowshed) was placed at the front or at the back of 'Awang Sang-goi', Chaboksang (quarter for delivery) was placed on the left side of the house. A quarter for the newly married couple (Ya-ongshang) was placed on the right side of the house. Foukei (grainary) was placed behind the 'Makha Sang-goi', Shingkei (quarter for fire wood) was placed on the right side of the house not far-away from Chaksang or the last room. Now such a maintenance of homestead has become a thing of the past. Chaboksang, Ya-ongshang, Shing-kei, Foukei, Yengkon, etc. are all disappeared. However, a house with 'Mamang Sang-goi' is still plenty in the rural areas of the valley. This is still found in some of the houses in Imphal also. But in the downtown area all these are missing and has no place in the urban set-up.

FIVE ROOMED HOUSE

In a five roomed house the open space at the front is Mang-gol (veranda). The Veranda is divided into Phamen and Naktha, etc. The second room is the place for sons and daughters. 'Ningolka' (quarter for the girls) is on the left side and 'Pibaka' (quarter for boys) is on the right side of the second room. The third room is the 'Phammenka', the place for the father. And opposite to it is the "Maibapham", the place for Maiba (the priest). The fourth room is the 'Laplenka', the place for the mother. The 'Fungga' or the hearth is placed at the centre of this room in front of the mother's bed. Opposite to the mother's bed is the place for the deity 'Leimaren'. The last room is the 'Laining-thouka'. In the south-western corner of this room there is seat for 'Sanamahi' deity. The Kitchen was not placed as an annexe. It was placed in the north–western corner of the last room.

MATERIALS USED IN THE TRADITIONAL HOUSE

Building materials were limited in number. They were tree, bamboo, reed, nail, chipped bamboo for binding (Paya), rope, rice straw, cow dung, sand, Leitan (clay), and Leimu (another type of clay) etc.

IMPLEMENTS

The implements used were: Hakmei, Shingjang (axe), Horai (saw), Thangjou (dagger), Paija (chisel), Thenggu, Leplei (screw auger), Guniya (Try square), Sang-gai, Thanggon (Sickle) and Ulum (weight). The Ulum was very simple and made by binding a piece of earth by a thread. The labelling was made from banana plant. Water is placed on the piece of banana plant blocked by mud on both the ends of it. The leaf of a plant named 'Heirit' was used in polishing the bamboo or the wood as we use 'sand paper' (polishing paper) in polishing wood or iron in present day's.

TIMING OF FELLING BAMBOO

There is a definite timing for felling the bamboo for building a house. In local calendar this is most suited in Mera-Hiyanggei (Oct. - Sept.). If it is cut beyond this two months then the bamboo becomes sweet. And insects (mite) can easily attack it. So, the most suitable month is Mera (October). Both the bamboo and wachet (chipped bamboo) are soaked in the water for some months, from one month to two and half months. This cannot be soaked in a longer period because the Wa and Wachet becomes weak again. Seasoning of the fine bamboo chip (paya) is done by soaking in the urine of cow. This means to protect it from insects. The other means is to place it above the hearth in the Kitchen or in the Fungga.

ARCHITECTURE OF YUMJAO

The building of a house begins with the lying of foundation. 'Yumpham' or the foundation was made by raising earth from nearby area or by digging a pond in the garden. The height of the 'Yumpham' depends upon the location of the place. It was two to three feet in height depending upon the water-level in the rainy season. It was on this 'Yumpham' that the whole structure of a Yumjao stood. The craftsman followed certain rules in building traditional houses which were partly technical and partly beliefs. The first pillar to be erected is the Urep (the main pillar or Jatra). This follows the positioning of twenty two (22) other major pillars. In between these major pillars a number of smaller pillars were erected which are known as 'Loy' depending upon the weight it has to carry.

NAME OF THE TWENTY TWO (22) MAJOR PILLARS

1. Saitin Atonba, Meiramgi Sum.
2. Loibi Charaihulpa, Loiyu Jatra.
3. Mabtao Ngaklou Ngaiba, Jatra Paba Loiyune (Emingthonggi Loiyu)
4. Langkheimanaoton, Langkhei Paba Loiyune.
5. Salthong Laimahalpa Sumne.
6. Emupham Lamsilpa, Laithangpa Ukokten.
7. Saruk Loutam Hulpa, Chakhumthangba Ukokten.
8. Pal-lem Naoyokpa, Koubru Thangba Sum. (Maningthonggi Loiyu).
9. Mongba Loiren Khomba, Awangthangba Loiyu.
10. Korou Nongchalpa, Maibaphamgi Loiyu.
11. Momnu Loutomba, Ningolka Loiyu.

12. Leirak Akhuba, Chingkhei Thangba Sum.
13. Eman Ngaina Namngou, Mangsok Ukokten.
14. Loklou Panam Enamkhang, Famlen Ukokten
15. Tareng.
16. Maipu.
17. Sentoppa, Faktom Puba Yumbi (3) Ahummak.
18. Langkhei Pungmayon, Chengfu U.
19. Langlel Kongyang Echeisu, Langchei.
20. Mongpasarong Laplenka, Sumang Yurangfam.
21. Mabtao Engngunungchalpa, Jatra Paba.
22. Langcheichara Yiruthek, Jatrane (Urep).

The position of the two pillars in the Veranda was determined not by architectural design but by traditional beliefs. The space between the right wall of the veranda and the pillar in the Phammen is wider than the space between the left wall of the veranda and the pillar in the Naktha. The belief embodies in this architecture is that the wider gap in the Phammen will bring fertility to family thereby increasing family members. The narrower gap in the Naktha is to lessen the frequent occurrence of death in the family. After positioning the pillars the first part to be put is the long Liokhangs or lower horizontal support beams. This follows the placing of other part, viz. Khangel (cross beam), Suktu (horizontal support beam), Akhuba (short support beam), Khongshangba (long vertical support), Khon.gtenba (short-leg vertical support), Thabakkhag Atenba (cross support beam), Thabakkhag Ashangba (lower cross support beam for roof).. Khangabu (upper support), Sanayumbi (vertical support for the main horizontal support beam), Yangbi (main horizontal beam), Yangnam (horizontal beam for securing the roof support) and Uchil-Lokpa, a runner above the

Thabakkhang supporting the hoomdang joining the two Segas.

After installing the frame the next step is to fix the Hoomdangs (lower roof support). While placing the Hoomdang over the Loikhang certain norms was followed which are based on the beliefs and customs as found in architectural lore. Wamit (eye) of the Hoomdang is not put facing down the ground but it is placed either on the left or right side.

The same is followed in erecting pillars. The wamit of the pillar is not placed facing inside the house. This is considered inauspicious. The number of Hoomdangs (in pairs) is determined by the size of the house and they are fixed in number. It is in the sense that they are to be of odd numbers. e.g.. 13, 15, 27, 23 etc. The way of counting is the use of (chak-rice, Nga-fish), or (Mei-fire, Eshing-water, Nungshit-air) or (chang-live, Shi-death) where chak-rice, Eshing-water and chang-live are considered auspicious. The Hoomdangs are not placed over the Loikhang in line with the pillars, however, this is relaxed in case of Laplen ka where a single Hoomdang is placed over the pillars which stands in the secluded area of 'Leimaren' deity. This is called "Ema Leimaren Shidabi Hoomdang Kokthong Pubi (Nabi)" - the literal meaning is that Ema-Leimarel Shidabi who carries the load of Hoomdang on the head. This gives us the concept of incorporating the symbol of sexual copulation in the architecture, thus cherishing the fertility cult. The placing of Hoomdangs begins from the back of house, not from the front. And it is finished at the front, however, it may finish at the left or right side of the front (Verandah). The belief is that when Man is created by God it begins from the buttock, thus enabling to identify whether the person is male or female. When placing the Ura (upper roof support made of polished bamboo splits) above the Hoomdangs there is not fixed numbers as it is there in the case of Hoomdangs. A thin bamboo chip is woven in between the U-ras at places which falls between the pair of Hoomdangs which is known as "Changkhrang". Its function is to reinforce the hold of the U-ras. The beliefs continues that Hoomdang represents the ribs, U-ras that of flesh and the thatch above the U-ras represents the skin. Funga-Lairu (the hearth) at the centre of the fourth room represents the navel of human beings. Among the major pillars there are eight (8) main pillars (for five-roomed house) which represents the eight (8) openings of the body. Again in a four-roomed house there are six (6) main pillars among the major pillars which represent the five souls and the shadow. Yangbi (main horizontal beam) which rests the Hoomdang and the U-ra at the top of the roof represent that of spinal cord. While placing the bamboo poles like Loikhang, Shuktu, Khangabu, Yangbi, etc. they are placed facing the head of the bamboo in the east.

They are personified as a sleeping man (Meitei) who is sleeping facing the east. The same is the case in erecting pillars also. If, otherwise, it is considered a man standing upside down which is believed inauspicious. While roofing with thatch sand is sprayed in between which acts as insulator in case of fire.

Plastering of the wall begins from placing the polished bamboo splits vertically and horizontally. In between it the materials Shingut (Phragmites) or Shingnang or Tou are inserted. This stage is known as "Kairangba". The first layer of plastering by mud is known as "Leipee". In this only mud and straw is used. The second layer is also by sand and cow dung. The third layer is also by sand and cow dung but in this sand is more in the proportion. Finishing is done by a fine layer of either Leitan (clay) or Leimu (another kind of clay).

DOORS AND WINDOWS

The main door is placed a little to the left, not in the centre or to the right. The back door is at the left wall of the last room. The passage beginning from the main door to the last room is kept open without any door. According to architectural lore the front door is known "Emangthong", and the back door is known as "Emingthong" respectively. There are two windows on both the sides of the main door. Windows are also made in the second, third, and fourth room, one each on the left and the right wall facing each other. The last room is without any window. "Thongnao" (window) is known Mihuthong" in the architectural lore.

SOME RULES

(a) Certain rule is followed in making holes for the pillars. The depth of a hole is determined by the distance between shoulder and the tip of male genital organ of the person (owner of the house). It can't be more than this.

(b) Shaichin or Shai (the lower end of the thatched-roof) should be elongated at least three (3) fts. from the pillars. This calculation is made by observing the inclination of rainfall in Manipur. If it is less than this the rains will reach the side veranda and the walls. There is no fixed heights of the houses. It depends on the desire of the person. A high house, is known as "Laba Yumsha" and the short one is known as "Amom Yumsha". However the difference is not much. It applies in the door also. A little broad door is known as "Amom Thongda" and a little higher is known as "Laba Thongda".

(c) Sanamahi ka -the room residing the deity Sanamahi should be made smaller than the other rooms.

(d) In the occurrence of death in the family the corpse is carried in the Ashithong (the space between the left pillar and the left wall of the veranda). If the member is a dying person he is carried in the centre of veranda i.e. passage between two pillars in the veranda. If death occurs when a marriage ceremony or death ceremony is undergoing in the family the corpse is passed by making a hole in the wall of the room " Phamen Ka". But this hole is made at the 'Khuya' (the back end of the person's bed) of the bed (i.e. on the right side of the wall).

(e) U-yung tree was excluded in building a house. It is believed that lightning will frequently visit the house.

Some Essential Accessories

Pungjei – It is a sharp pointed bamboo splits which acts as nails. It is believed that it represents the male genital organ.

Pandali – It is the binding with cane splits. It is used in two places, one-between Kbangabu and Yangbi, two between Loikhang and Loikhom.

Hirukhang – It is like Pungjei but it is longer upto 1/2 ft. to 2 ft. It is made by sharpening the bamboo split, specially from the head of the bamboo split including the wamit (eye) and is pointed toward the end of the split. It is driven home upto the end with a wooden hammer (Tokshu) at the "Shaijin" (the lower edge of the thatched roof). The purpose is to fasten the hold of the thatch in the U-ras.

Saikhang – A polished bamboo chip which is fastened at the eaves by the support of Hirukhang.

Sega – A wooden pole inserted in between the joints of U-ras of main part of the house and that of veranda.

Yengai – Yengai or Shandangkha is a triangular bamboo weave structure placed above the front wall of the house but below the roof to serve as ventilator. It is decorated with flowers, birds, house and other motifs carved from bamboo chips by fixing among the interlacing weaves.

SOME PRACTICES

SHAGUN THONG

(passage for the burglar) : In the traditional practice a passage for the burglar known as 'Shagun Thong' was also included in the architecture. The belief around this practice is that if the burglar eats something before stealing the belongings then he stops stealing. So, he eats only when he collects whatever he likes. By so doing the act will cast spell to the sleeping members of the .family. If such an act happens the usual belief is that the act of burglary will repeat again. The burglar usually escapes at the passage (Shagun Thong). If the burglar intends to make the owner rich he will escape by the front door.

Shag un Thong Thingba : The burglar after executing his mission escapes at the passage (Shagun Thong). But, sometimes he will note escape immediately along with the stolen articles. He will block the passage by the earth around it. If such an act happens it is usually believed that the family will get rich in the days to come. On the other hand it is also considered that the burglar left something for the survival of the family.

Shenfu : A locker for the coins was also prepared by making a small hole in one of the secluded pillar, usually near one of the household deity. The hole is made at the upper edge of the joint. When it is desired to remove then another hole is made at the lower end of the joint of the piliar.

In due course of time traces of modernisation is found in the architecture of Yumjao. Shikhong (a horizontal plank at the basement) and Pheiren (another plank criss-crossing the wall) are the latter additions in the architecture. The bamboo supports and pillars also began to be replaced by wooden ones. With this the wooden pillars are placed above fine polished square shaped stones instead of inserting pillars in the earth. However, the Hoomdang (lower rpof support), the U-ra (the upper roof support), and the thatched roof survived the changes. Again a bamboo pillar among the wooden pillars was retained in the south-western corner of the house where a secluded place is reserved for the household deity - 'Sanamahi'.

With the arrival of modernisation the traditional houses are gradually replaced by modern concrete structures. However, the replacement is not sudden and there is a transitional stage. In this transitional stage the bamboo is completely replaced by wood along with the architectural design. However, the plastering of the wall is still done by mud and the final plastering is done by white washing. The thatched roof is also replaced by tin roof. In both the transitional house and modern concrete structures the hearth, the Yengai and the place for the deity "Leimaren" is missing. However, in both the cases a secluded place for the supreme household deity "Sanamahi" is still reserved with renewed enthusiasm.

DEITIES IN THE HOUSE

In a traditional Yumjao a number of places inside the house were reserved for a number of deities ranging from the three principal deities e.g. Lainingthou Sanamahi, Ema Leimarel Shidabi and Emoinu to other minor deities e.g. Saijin Polibi, Santhong Apanba, Thongaren, etc. However, such reserved places were more distinct for the above three principal deities and for the remaining minor deities their places were more or less based on beliefs. For the moment the study is concentrated mostly on the three principal deities.

SANAMAHI

To begin with the place for Lainingthou Sa nama hi is reserved at the south-western corner of the last room which is known as "Lainingthou Ka" – meaning room for the "Lainingthou. This room is also known as "Chak-Khum Ka", meaning room for Kitchen. Sanamahi is worshipped everyday in the evening by offering Mekruk (traditional incense) and light. But special offering is made on 'Cheiraoba'- Manipuri New Year day. On this day a variety of vegetables, fruits and flowers which are available in the season are offered as "Athenpot". On the day of 'Cheiraoba' or during the five days beginning from it the old clothes of 'Sanamahi' is replaced by a set of new clothes which is known as 'Firoi Hongba'. Sanamahi is also worshipped occasionally by an indiviaual when there is a desire to get an offspring or when one wants to cure someone from insanity. The auspicious month for such a worship is "Enga'-July and the auspicious day is "Thanin"- the full moon day. However, with the advent of modern education and scientific knowledge such practices are gradually discarding in the society.

LEIMAREN

The place for 'Leimaren' is reserved at the left side of "LaplenKa"- the room for the mother (housewife) of the family. 'Leimaren' is also prayed everyday in the evening by offering Mekruk and light. Special offering is made on the day of "Cheiraoba"- the new year day. "Phiroi Hongba"- change of new clothes is also performed during the five days beginning from "Cheiraoba". During these five days the water in the 'Eshaifu'- the earthen pitcher, is also replaced by a fresh one. But the water is collected from seven (7) 'Hiden'- the bathing place in a river. On special occasions "Leimaren" is also worshipped not exceeding once in a month. Even the king cannot go beyond this practice. If it is worshipped twice a month it was believed that the country will face a catastrophe. A host of item is included in such occasional prayer.

EMOINU

Like the above two deities "Emoinu" is also prayed everyday in the evening. Her place is located just near the "Funga Lairu" (the hearth), but on its south-western side. A small mound is placed at this place to mark the location of Emoinu. Whatever cooked in the family was also offered both in the morning and evening. Like the above two principal deities 'Emoinu' is also worshipped en masse on 12th day of Wakching month (equivalent to January). For such an occasional worship two 'Athenpots' are prepared which includes fruits, flowers, vegetables and other items which are available in the season. One Athenpot is offered to 'Funga Lairu' and the other to 'Lainingthou Sanamahi'. The offering is often accompanied with the chanting of 'Nahairon'. The items included in 'Nahairon' are Tairen, Pungfai, Napu, Nashet, Napi and Shingbi. These are dipped in water and sprinkled the nearby area including the. 'Athenpot'. Only Tairel leaf is used in 'Nahaiba' when the other items are not available.

REFERENCES

1. *Yumsharon - MS.*
2. *Sanamahi Phangkhong - MS.*
3. *Leimaren Sekning - MS.*
4. *Leimaren Naoyom - MS.*
5. *Leimaren Phambal- MS.*
6. *Sanamahi Phambal - MS.*
7. *Oral interview with Ph. Achou of Andro Mamang Leikai.*
8. *Oral interview with (Craftsman) Kh. Thambalngou.*
9. *Oral interview with Ksh. Boro Singh.*
10. *Oral interview with Pt. N. Manijao.*
11. *Emoinu Ahongbigi Likhul Pomit - Y Budhichandra.*
12. *Cane and Bamboo crafts of Manipur - Mutua Bahadur.*

3

TERMS OF ADDRESS WITHIN THE KINSHIP AND OUTSIDE

In addressing a person of consanguineous relation or a person related due to marriage the sound E is prefixed. For example, Epa, for father, Eyamba for elder brother and Eche for elder sister, etc. This is applied to a person who is related due to marriage. As for instance Ebai for brother-in-law, Enempok for mother-in-law and Ekupok for father-in-law, etc. However, due to contact with Hindu culture a change is observed in the traditional terms of address. And the change goes in this way: Baba for father, Dada for elder brother, Khura for uncle, etc. The traditional terms of address is a close knitted one and the use of prefix 'E' implies a close blood relationship among the persons of consanguineous relation or relation developed due to marriage.

The terms of address among the consanguineous relation and the relation developed out of marriage can be examined in the following manner:

Epa – Father, addressed by both man and woman to man.

Ema – Mother, addressed by both man and woman to woman

Epan – This is addressed to father's elder

brothers and mother's sister's husband. This term can also be applied to mother-in-Iaw's brother if he is older than one's father. This is addressed by both man and woman to man. Now in place of Epan, Pajihan, Pabunghan, Pabungyaima, etc,. are also used to denote eldest, elder Epan.

Eton, Khura - Uncle. – This is addressed to father's brothers and mother's younger sister's husband. Eton is used in showing relationship and as well as in addressing. Likewise khura also has the same implication. Thus Eton, Khura is used in addressing a man younger than one's -father whether related by blood or not. This is addressed by both man and woman to man. In place of Eton or Kaka is increasingly using in these days.

Mamma – This is addressed to father's younger or elder sister's husband and mother's elder and younger brothers. Mamhan is addressed to both father's elder sister's husband and mother's elder brother. Mamma is addressed to father-in-law's younger brother which is also addressed as Ekuton. Mamma is addressed by both man and woman to man.

Eku – This is addressed by a person to his father-in- law and by a woman to her father-in-law. 'Ekuhan' is addressed to elder brother of father-in-law and

Ekuyaima, Ekuton to younger brothers of fatherin-law. This is addressed by both man and woman to man. But now-a-days this is hardly used. A man addresses Paji or Pabung or Baba to his father-in-law. Likewise a woman also addresses Paji or Pabung or Baba to her father-in-law.

Emhan – This is addressed to father's elder brother's wife and mother's elder sisters. In short wife of Epans are Emhans. This is addressed by man and woman to woman.

Ene, Enem – This is addressed to both father's elder and younger sisters as well as to mother's elder and younger brother's wives. 'Enehan' is addressed to elder and 'Eneton' to younger one. This is also addressed to father-in-law. Nowadays' Enempok' is reduced to showing relationship not in addressing. This is often replaced by 'Ema'-Mother. Ene, Enem is addressed by both man and woman to woman.

Endon – This is addressed to wives of Khuras, Etons , mother's younger sisters and mother-in-law's younger brother's wife. This is addressed by both man and woman to woman. 'Endomcha'is often used in place of 'Endon'.

Tada, Eyamba, Ebung – Tada or Eyamba is addressed to elder brothers, father's brother's elder sons, wife's elder sister's husband, and to husband's elder sister's husband. All the elder sons of Khuras and Epans are Tada or Eyambas. Tada is used by both man and woman to man whereas Eyamba is used by man to man. The use of Tada seems to be of recent origin which may be a derivative of Hindu Culture. A woman addresses 'Ebung' to their elder brothers and father's elder sons. With the increasing use: of Tada in place of 'Ebung', 'Ebung' is now reduced to showing relationship rather than addressing. Tada or Eyamba is also used to elder persons who are outside kinship relationship. And hence they are used in showing kinship relationship as well as in addressing. As for instance, in addressing an elder the word Tada is prefixed to one's name, i.e. Tadachaoba, etc.

Enao – Enao is often used in showing relationship but less in addressing someone. They are often call by name. Enao is addressed to younger brothers, wife's younger sisters husband, all the younger sons of Khuras and Epans (man to man), husband's younger brother's and to maternal uncle's younger sons (woman to man). This is also addressed to one's younger sisters, all the younger daughters of Khuras and Epans and to husband's younger brother's wife {woman to woman).

Ebai – Ebai is addressed to one's wife's brothers, elder sister's (including father's brother's elder daughter's) husband and to father' sister's elder sons. This is used to all the elder sons of Mamma's and Ene's. This is addressed by man to man.

Eshen – Eshen is addressed to all the younger brother of the above relationship. This is used in addressing man to man. But Eshen is often used in showing relationship but less in addressing. For addressing one uses the name of the person.

Eteima – Eteima is addressed by man to woman. This is addressed to elder brother's wife, Khuras's and Epan's elder son's wife, wife's elder sisters, mother's brother's elder daughters and,to father's sister's elder daughter. This is also addressed to all the elder daughters of Mammas and Enes.

Enaonupi – This is addressed to all the younger of the above relationship (man to woman). And this is also addressed to wife's younger sisters, husband's younger brother's wife, and to younger sisters (including father's brother's younger, i.e. younger daughters of Khuras and Epans). This is also used in addressing woman to woman. 'Enaonupi' is often used in showing relationship not in addressing someone. In addressing them they are often called by names.

Etei – This is used in addressing woman to man. Etei is addressed to one's husband's elder brothers, father-in-Iaw's brother's elder sons and to father's sister's elder sons. Eteihan, Eteiyaima is used to the eldest and elder Etei. But the present trend is to call by name to 'Eteis' with the prefix of Tada.

Eche – Eche is addressed by both man and woman to woman. This is addressed to elder sisters, elder daughters of Epans and Khuras and to wife of Ebai (man to woman). Again this is addressed to elder sisters as in the above and to husband's elder brother's wife, i.e. wife of Etei (woman to woman).

Echan – This is addressed to younger sisters including father's brother's younger daughters, i.e. younger daughters of Epans and Khuras and to wife of Eshen (man to woman). This is also addressed to a woman's younger brother's wife and to husband's younger sisters (woman to woman). Echan is also mostly used in showing relationship but less in addressing.

Enama – This is used in addressing woman to woman. This is addressed to elder's brother's wife. Khura's and Epan's elder son's wife, husband's elder sisters, husband's father's brother's elder daughters, and to mother's brother's elder daughters. 'Enamahan' is the eldest of the 'Enamas'.

Emou – This is used mostly in showing relationship rather than addressing. This is used in addressing man to woman and woman to woman. Son's wife, brother's son's wife and sister's daughters are 'Emous' (man to woman). Son's wife, husband's brother's son's wife and husband's sisters daughters are also 'Emous' (woman to woman). 'Emous' are often called by name.

Echa – Likewise 'Emou', Echa is used in showing relationship not in addressing .They are called by name. 'Echa' comprises sons and daughters, brother's children, wife's sister's children, husband's brother's children and sister's children. They are addressed by man to woman and woman to man.

Epwa – 'Epwa' is also used in showing relationship. When calling them they are called by name. Younger brother, younger sons of khuras and Epans and husband's younger sister's husband are referred as 'Epwa' (woman to man)

Emak – 'Emak' is used in showing relationship not in addressing a person. Daughter's husband including those of brother's daughter's, sister's son and wife's brother's son are referred as 'Emak' (man to man). 'Emaks' are often called by name.

Eya – 'Eya' is also used in showing relationship rather than addressing a person. They are often called by name. Daughter's husband, husband's brother's daughters husband, husband's sister's sons and brother's sons are referred as 'Eyas' (woman to man)

Eshu – 'Eshu' is also used in showing relationship not in, addressing. When calling them they are called by name. 'Eshu' is grandson and grand daughter. Children of son's and daughters are'Eshu'. Children of sons, daughters of Khuras and Epans and children of sister's son and daughter are also 'Eshu'.

Epu, Epubok, Epudhou – "Epu' or 'Epubok' is grandfather. This is addressed by both man and woman to man. 'Epudhou' is great grandfather and this is also addressed by both man and woman to man.

Eben, Ebenpok, Ebenthou – 'Eben' or 'Ebenpok' is grand mother. And is addressed by both man and woman to woman. 'Ebenthou' is great grandmother (man and woman to woman).

Purennakakpa – It is the seventh generation counting backward from father. This is rather used ironically. He is almost equivalent to a Shagei's Pukok (progenitor).

REFERENCES

1. Minggou Thagou - MS.
2. Oral interview with Ph. Achou of Andro Mamang Leikai.
3. Oral interview with M. Thabal of Wangkhei Angom Leikai.
4. Notes on Meithei (Manipuri) beliefs and customs, J.C. Higgins (I.C.S), Vice-President, Manipur State Darbar. Edited by John Parratt -1998.

4

YUPAN THABA (BIRTH CEREMONY)

In Andro the birth ceremony is held as 'Yupan Thaba' either on the fifth day or sixth day of the birth of the child depending on the sex of the child. For male it is held on the fifth day whereas for female the same is held on the sixth day. However, the ritual offering begins on the day before the actual day of 'Yupan Thaba'. So in the evening of the day before' Yupan Thaba', i.e. on the fourth day for male and fifth day for female a small offering is made to deity. Such an offering is made on headside of the child's bed. The items include rice, egg, fruits and betel nuts and leaves. A seat for the deity is made on the ground by placing a small 'Khudei' (loin cloth) which is known as 'Phambal'. Above the 'Phambal' a piece of banana leaf is placed. And on it rice, Thoiding (Til), three buds of Phungphai (a grass) and a few flowers are placed for offering. Alongside the 'Phambal' a 'Meruk' (measuring pot for rice meant for cooking) full of rice is also placed. And on the rice an egg is placed. Around it ' Heiruk Tanga' (Shared fruits) and 'Pana Tanga' (Shared betel nut and leaves) are also placed. In the midst of such offerings a piece of paper and a pen is also inserted. However, the inclusion of such items is influenced by the belief that the future of the child is kept written by the Almighty on the piece of paper. But this is a belief only and it never happens. Such a practice strongly assures us that the Andro community has a strong sense of fetishism. Birth record is not popular in Andro; however, the year, month, day and the time of birth is kept in their memory.

On the day of 'Yupan Thaba' which is held either on the fifth or sixth day the offering is made in the verandah. It is a simple ritual which is centred around the offering of "Phoudang Phou' - a basket full of paddy. The paddy is kept filled in a basket known as 'Likhai'. A garland of dried fish of 'Ngakha' or 'Phabou' is placed above the paddy. Along with it a pair of coin and a pair of 'Meitei Thum' (local salt prepared in the form of a plate) are placed on the basket. The offering include 'Waiyu' (rice bear) which is placed near the basket. Now-a-days 'Waiyu' is replaced by 'Kalei' (strong liquor) as preparing 'Waiyu' is time consuming and laborious. The preparation of 'Phoudang Phou' is the work of the concerned family and is done without the direction of 'Maibi'.

The offering is accompanied by a short prayer by both the 'Maibi' and the family members, particularly women of the family. After this short prayer a feast exclusively arranged and organised by women of the family and the neighbourhood is held. However, the bathing of the child and the mother precedes the feast. The child is carefully bathed by the 'Maibi'. The bathing of the mother, however, depend on the health condition of the mother.

Next to 'Maibi Chaklon Katpa', 'Yupan Thaba' is also another all women affair. But in this occasion in any context man is excluded from the scene. Depending upon the condition of the family a number of women from the neighbourhood are invited for the ceremony. Men are excluded from the invitation. The invitation essentially includes the 'Maibi' (priestess cum medical practitioner), Maiyoknabi (assistant to Maibi) and Khom-enbi (the breast feeder). These three women are necessarily involved in the delivery of the child where 'Maibi' plays main part in labour work and she is assisted by the 'Maiyoknabi'. The 'Khomenbi' feeds the baby from her breast not from the mother of the baby on the delivery day. The tradition of inclusion of 'Khom-enbi' is solely from the belief that the mother's milk in the early days of the birth of the baby is considered unfit for consumption. So for many hundreds of years together the people of this place has not been using the best part of mother's milk which is fully nutritious and a source of the child's immunity. Considering the crucial role of the three women in the delivery of the baby where a minor negligence may lead to the fatality of the baby, their invitation in the feast is nothing less than a gratitude to them for their invaluable service to the family. All the invited women of the neighbourhood attend the ceremony with a chicken in their hands. The host family also shares a number of necessary chickens for the feast along with the necessary items in cooking. So the involving women; they contribute, they cook and they dine together in the feast.

Before sitting for the feast they share a round of their local liquor. Sometimes excessive rounds make someone loosing her balance.

In fact this is a short of merry-making in the ceremony. But to a family with unsound financial position such a feast and merry-making is simply avoided. While enjoying the feast the 'Maibi' is elevated to a certain status which is marked by the specific share of the cook which necessarily includes different parts of a chicken such 'Makan', Makel (liver), a leg of the chicken, a wing, the shoulder and the head of the chicken. Traditionally this is known as "Shaga-Ngaka". This share of the 'Maibi' is a must in such a ceremony. The 'Maibi' can finish her share at the feast itself or she has the option to carry it at her home. The male members of the family are not allowed to dine at the feast together with the invited women, instead a separate place is arranged for them.

At the point of departure after the feast the 'Maibi' is offered a sum of Rs. 50/- or Rs. 100/- as an honour of her service to the family in respect of the delivery of the baby and the subsequent birth ceremony. However, this is not simply an act of handing over and taking over the offered money, here also the 'Maibi' will go away after forecasting something for the family. She performs an observation known as " Shenmit Yengba". The money offered in notes is wrapped along with a few coins in three layers by pieces of banana leaves. The bund i.e., bundle is now tied by any available article; thread or creeper, etc. The same is now hit on the ground and in the process the 'Maibi' predicts the sex of the next baby of the same mother.

YUMSHENGBA

This ceremony is a component of the birth ceremony. The brief ritual is based on the belief that the birth of the baby pollute the house and subsequently needs purifying the house. So 'Yumshengba' is nothing but the act of purifying the house which is held on the third day of the birth of the baby. Even these days the belief has its firm footing. The act of purifying the house is performed by the 'Maibi' who laboured in the delivery of the baby. The 'Maibi' visits the house in the morning. She uses 'Tairen' (leaf of a tree) leaves and holy water in purifying the house. However, she follows a procedure in purifying the house. She begins from the secluded place of 'Lainingthou Sanamahi' the supreme household deity and goes through the different rooms of the house and finally terminates at the verandah of the house. She dips the 'Tairen' leaves in the holy water and sprinkle it at every place of house with the words "On this third day I have cleaned the polluted elements from the house". At the end the 'Tairen' leaves are kept inserted at the eaves dropper of the house.

Again on this day of 'Yumshengba' for the first time the baby is fed by the milk of the mother. This day is marked as *"Khomdin Numit".*

CHAK-UMBA

Chak-Umba, the rice feeding ceremony is held when the baby is three months old. It is held in the morning. For this an auspicious day is selected. On this day the mother feeds the baby with a soft fish when the sun appears on the horizon. It is a simple ceremony and only the mother perform it. Both the male and female baby is held on completion of three months. There are families which include the offering of fruits and betel nuts and leaves. But this is done under the influence of Meitei Hindus.

REFERENCES

1. Oral interview with Chingakham Thambal - on 16th March, 2006.
2. Oral interview with Sarubam Lalito - Andro Khunou Leikai.
3. Oral interview with Sarubam Ongbi Dharmomala Devi.

5

KINSHIP AND MARRIAGE

Traditionally three kinds of marriage is practised in Andro which are (a) Hainaba, (b) Chelhong and (c) Kaina Katpa. Among them Hainaba, engagement form of marriage is the most p:opular one. And it involves a long process, spanning even years to reach the final day of marriage. In Andro society the boys were given the right to make a choice of his own mate. But his aspiration could be fulfilled through engagement form of marriage as elopement was considered as breach of custom and had to face the wrath of the community. Monogamous marriage is the only popular form of marriage. Polygamous is quite unpopular in Andro society. All the rituals and ceremonies of existing types of marriages revolve around engagement form of marriage. Whereas other forms of marriage is the transformation in one way or the other from this principal marriage form. It involves a long process and the tradition is also very old. The essence of rituals in marriage remain unchanged through the ages, although there are some minor changes in dress, container used, etc. Engagement could be done with mutual consent of the boy and girl or without the knowledge of them; done mostly by the parents. Though engagement needs a long process to be followed but still this is in fashion.

STAGES IN ENGAGEMENT FORM OF MARRIAGE

The task of engagement begins with the selection of an influential elderly person from the Leikai (locality). The parents of the boy persuade the elderly person (a male) to bear the responsibility for engagement along with difficulties that may appear in the event of execution of the task. The elderly man acceded to the strong persuasion of the boy's parents. And finally on an auspicious day he visits the girl's parents. He is welcomed there as usual with the offering of pipe smoke, etc. The girl's parents enquire on the purpose of his visit. On this first encounter he will not divulge his purpose candidly, but hinted them that the boy's parents ask the most precious asset from your family for the boy. And thus he leaves the girl's house.

The statement of the elderly man awaken the slumber of the parents. And thus works to decode the statement. Finally the parents converges that the elderly man is asking the hand of their daughter for the particular boy. So the parents undergo investigation about the boy as well as the boy's parents. As a custom the elderly man will visit the girl's parents for the second time and everyone is aware of this.

For the second time the old man visits the girl's parents after some weeks or some months. This time the elderly man candidly declares his proposal of engagement of the girl. This time also the elderly man returns home after giving ample time to the girl's parents for a reply of the proposal.

The second visit of the elderly man brings additional seriousness of the parents. Degree of consultation increases in the girl's parents. The father seeks the opinion of the mother and the mother for the girl through her girl friends. Before arriving a decision among the parents and the girl they also study the boy, his parents and his locality. Now the matter is thrown open for discussion in the kin of the father with the inclusion of at least three elderly persons of the neighbourhood. However, the opportunity for the final decision is left to the parents.

For the third and final round the elderly person visit the parents. This time also he presents his early proposal. In the event of certain reservation by the girl's parents the elderly man exerts his strongest persuasion till the parents agrees his proposal. And the elderly man returns home with the agreed proposal.

The role of the elderly man do not end here. Soon he once again visit the girl's parents and formally intimate the day of 'Haijapot'- the first ceremony in engagement form of marriage where the affair of the two families is make known to the public formally. The elderly man returns home leaving behind the day for 'Haijapot' as another proposal to the girl's parents. The father of the girl gives his reply by visiting the house of the boy after duly considering all aspects of the day. And thus decides the day of 'Haijapot'.

Haijapot Puba (The Ceremony Haijapot)

The ceremony is carried out with a brief ritual. For this 'Athenpots' are prepared with fruits and sweets like 'Kabok' (puffed rice), Kangshubi, Kwa (betel nut and leaves), Chu (cane sugar), banana, etc. These 'Athenpots" are meant for offering to deities (household) 'Lainingthou' and 'Leimaren'.

In addition to these 'Athenpots' fruits and sweets are also arranged for the gathering at the girl's house. These items are to be carried by male and female members of the locality. Included in the procession are the relatives and friends of the boy's father.

The actions of the persons gathering in the ceremony is bound and regulated by certain customs of the community. The women of the boy's side who has carried the Athenpots cannot go straight inside the house of the girl to offer to 'Lainingthou' and 'Leimaren'. They are received by women of girl's side at the verandah of the house and they are the one who is to offer to the deities. Seats are provided for the old ones from 'the boy's side at the 'Phammen' of the Verandah (right side of Verandah) while others are allowed to sit in other areas of the house. What immediately followed is the exchange of bowing offered by boy's father and his entourage. After offering the 'Athenpots' what is 'brought from the boy's side is distributed to all those present in the gathering. In this stage also the social institution of the village is involved. The distribution is supervised by 'Shingjuba' (Shinshuba) of the Leikai (locality) where he is assisted by the boys of the Leikai. In the past he was empowered to punish anyone absent in the ceremony.

As a custom persons from boy's side were not allowed to take part in the distribution of the sweets and fruits. The ceremony ends with another round of bowing between the parents of boy's and girl's side. The exchange of bowing, especially between the fathers of boy's and girl's is known as 'Ngai Sen Konnaba' in traditional jargon.

Waroipot

The next step followed after 'Haijapot' is 'Waroipot'. In the case of 'Haijapot' the day was fixed by the joint effort of the boy's and girl's parents. But on the occasion of 'Waroipot' the matter is left open to the boy's parents. So the day is fixed according to the convenience of the boy's parents. However, all this is depended on the financial position of the boy's parents. Generally, 'Waroipot' is held in the next year, not in the same year with 'Haijapot'. But this can also be held in the same year if the boy's parents can afford it.

Ingredients

With the advance in stage of engagement there arises difference in ingredients in between 'Haijapot' and 'Waroipot'. Like 'Haijapot' sweets, fruits like Kabok (puffed rice),

Kangshubi (local sweet), Kwa (betel nuts and leaves), sugar cane, banana and other available fruits are carried on this day also. 'Athenpots' are also prepared for the household deities out of the above items. In addition the carried items are meant for those present on the occasion. However, the difference crops up with the addition of the two items i.e. 'Yu'(local liquor) and meat or fish (cooked one) . 'Yu' was excluded in 'Haijapot' but now this is deliberately included in 'Waroipot'. And here arises the significance of 'Yu' in the cultural life of the 'Andros'. There is hardly any ritual in 'Andro' where 'Yu' is not included. Here 'Yu' is not only for the deities, this is also meant for those present on the occasion. However, the distribution of the 'Yu' is the task of the boys of the girl's 'Leikai"(locality).

On the other side if meat or fish is included in the carried items then 'Athenpots' of either meat or fish are also carried to the girl's home. After accomplishing this ritual 'Waroipot' the girl is not allowed to elope to another boy nor she cannot be engaged to another person. This occasion makes public that the girl has been engaged to the boy. And all those present are the witnesses of the occasion. If the girl elopes to another boy after 'Waroipot' then she will be fined. Previously there was a fix rate for such a fine and it differs with the stage of engagement. If the girl elopes after 'Haijapot' she was fined Rs. 400/-. And Rs. 500/- was the rate if she does after 'Waroipot'. However, at present the rate has been revised and its begins with Rs. 1000/-. In the ancient past when money economy was not popular, the fine might be in kind, most probably by a pig. Because in most of the societies pig was considered as the most suitable animal for the payment of fine, etc. Pig is useful only for food item and they are not helpful in agriculture and other economic activities. Other animals like cows and buffaloes are more useful in view of their engagement in many economic activities. So this might be one reason why cows and buffaloes are excluded in using them as fine in such cases.

Now attitudes are changed and in such changed environment the girl's side may press-to include meat in the items for 'Waroipot'. In such a situation the boy's side cannot escape and ought to include meat in the array of items. The meat is not raw one, but it is a cooked one, to be cooked by boy's side. However, the meat is not a well-cooked food, it is cooked only to remove the blood-stain. Such a meat is first offered to the household deities, to 'Lainingthou' and 'Leimarel' and to 'SharoiNgaroi' at the gate of the house. After this offering and prayer the meat is shared to all those present and relish it.

In such an occasion the locality i.e. the society is involved, and the social institution 'Shingjuba' performs its role as an organiser cum arranger. 'Shingjuba' is the corrupt of 'Shinshuba'- the one who arranges and organises. The 'Shingjuba' commands the team (boys) of the locality who performs the simple orderly works. The task may be simple but one cannot play truant in his participation. 'Shingjuba' has a wonderful piece of knowledge and he can easily point out the absentees. And he is empowered to punish the absentees. The engagement of the boys to such simple task lays the foundation for their promotion to higher institutions like 'Arangpham' and 'Pujari' of the village. In one sense the boys are given elementary education (social) before promoting to higher institutions.

Laipot

It is a form of package food to be made by cooked pig. As suggested by the name the package is meant to be offered to household deities, i.e. 'Sanamahi' and 'Leimarel'. In 'Laipot'; 'Lai' is deity and 'Pot' is anything to be offered. So such a package food is generally offered in 5 or 7 or 9 in numbers to the deities. But the service do not end here and proceeds further. And one has to prepare 80 to 90 'Laipot' and sometimes more than 100, this time for the relatives of the brides family. And all these are prepared and presented by the boy's side to the girl's side. Traditionally 'Laipot' was prepared by pork. But now-a-days fish, both row and dry, is gradually replacing the pork. The reason is not far to seek, economic factor has compelled them to turn to fish. But one cannot prepare 'Laipot' by fish and meat together, A hand of banana and 'Kabok' (puffed rice) supplement either fish or meat in preparing the packet. However, 'Kabok' is excluded if the 'Laipot' is made of meat. The Andros maintain certain code in killing the pig but such a binding is not there in the case of fish. They observe 'E :Khudeng' and 'Lai Khudeng' days. And they will kill the pig on 'Lai Khudeng' day. 'E Khudeng' day is considered inauspicious and 'IE, Khudeng' day is considered auspicious. As a custom the number of 'Laipot' is determined by the bride's parents. If the bride's parents do not want to trouble the groom's parents then they can advise the boy's side to prepare 'Laipot' for the deity only, i.e. 5 or 7 or 9. If on the other side the bride's parents want to tame the high handedness of the boy's side they can order a maximum number of 'Laipot' even crossing a hundred. The remaining 'Laipots', after offering 5 or 7 or 9 to the deities, are distributed to the relatives of the girl. And those relatives who has received the same will return presents in the form of metal jar (Korphu) and broad plates (Kompak). Such presents known as 'Potpang' will gather in the girl's house in large numbers. Presents in such utensils has immense value in Andro till date. Because such jars are used in preparing 'Yu', the local liquor which is still treated as a source of income. In the past such jars might be of earthen one. But now-a-days metal jars are gradually replacing the earthen one. Such presents will help in establishing the new family. Lastly 'Laipot' is carried on 'Waroipot' and Heijingpot'. The presence of 'Laipot' on the day of 'Waroipot' gives ample time to her relatives to prepare the present.

Luhongba (Heijingpot-Marriage)

Now after much engagements, parleys and diplomatic efforts the final stage of marriage "Luhongba" is arrived. And this is the stage where the two sides are brought closer to one another. The tradition of Andro spells that the day for marriage cannot be decided by anyone from boy's or girl's side. And this is to be decided by an astrologer. Either of the boy's side or girl's side alone cannot go to the astrologer, but both the parents of the boy's and girl's will approach the astrologer. And they will make a fervent request for an auspicious day for the marriage. 'Andros' do not have the tradition of maintaining 'Kosthi' - the birth record. They do not maintain their birth record properly. Instead they have an oral tradition. What they do is to remember the name of the Cheithaba (record keeper) at the palace when the person is born. Thus they do not have the knowledge of the month, day and time of the birth of the person. And what they remember is the name of the 'Cheithaba' the chronicle recorder and thus they reveal the date of birth of the child or person. Now comes the turn of the astrologer and he will examine whether there is 'Luhongphal' for the boy or not. 'Luhongphal'- its literal meaning is the wooden seat used on the day of marriage meant for sitting by the groom at the courtyard. But in this context it means the auspicious day for the marriage of the boy. And thus the astrologer decides the day and month of 'Luhongphal' of the boy. So the auspicious day and month of marriage is given by the astrologer. Here in deciding the auspicious day a gender inequality is visible. There is no tradition of finding an auspicious or inauspicious day from the girl side. This is due to the subservient position of women in Andro society in particular and Meitei society in general. Simply a girl or a women is not-counted as a person at par with a normal man. Again the marriage cannot be held if there is not 'Luhongphal' for the boy. He has to wait till his auspicious day. Availability of 'Luhongphal' do not end with an individual, such a situation prevails in the village level also. For the Andro village the 'Wakching' (January) month is a taboo month for marriage. Marriage is forbidden in this month. No specific reason is assigned to this custom. Unlike 'Enga' (June) and 'Engel' (July) which are heavily engaged in cultivation, 'Wakching' is a relatively free month, free from hectic engagement of cultivation. Again it is a month which has a good stock of food harvested from the labour of Enga-Engel (June, July). When there is not any rite and ritual in Enga-Engel (June, July) the reason is not far to trace. Not to mention of rites and rituals, even the ailing person, the saying goes, is kept covered by 'Foura'- a flat basket meant for drying paddy in the sun. It implies that even an ailing person is kept unattended during this two months due to the high intensity of engagement in the field. What is interesting here is the attitude of a group of people or a community to deities involving rites and rituals and even to ailing person depending on the climatic condition of a region and the nature of the economy.

From the above discussion it is evident that engagement form of marriage, though the most popular form of marriage, involves a long process with the direct or indirect engagement of a number of people. And it is less economical. Such a lengthy process is abruptly shortened if the girl is eloped. If the parents favours the girl's action the marriage can be held without much delay. But such an action has no social sanction and the Andro society consider it a breach of custom. So most of the parents count it as an insult to them. If the parents want to teach a lesson to their daughter the marriage can be delayed as long as they desire. In such a situation the boy's parents has to request the girl's parents time and again for the marriage. Marriage through elopement is known as 'Chelhong' in Manipuri and it involves a brief ceremony. This will be discussed in the later part.

Bor Barton Touba

In between 'Waroipot' and 'Heijingpot' (Luhongba-marriage) there is a custom of inviting the Bar (groom) known as 'Bor Barton Touba'. It is generally held on the day before the marriage. The persons involved are a boy, preferably the youngest brother of the girl and the 'Arangba' (the arranger) of the locality. In the past 'Arangba' alone went for the invitation. The inclusion of a boy is a recent phenomenon. To be more exact the invitation is from the girl side, the girl is inviting the boy (the groom) requesting him to present in the marriage ceremony. The groom dresses up with 'Feijom' (dhoti) and 'Pumyat' (Kurta, Shirt) as if he dresses on the day of marriage; and waits for the invitation. The boy invites the Bor (groom) by handing over fruits, betel nuts and leaves, etc. The groom receives the invitation by his own hand. This the boy does by bowing to the groom. This 'Bor Barton Touba' seems to be an addition to Meitei society after the adoption of Hinduism as State religion. And later the adoption had its influence to Andro society. Basically the Andros resisted the forced conversion into Hinduism by the King of Manipur. However, later on the changed religion in the bigger society had its influence to the smaller communities. The practice 'Bor Barton Touba' seems to be against the tradition of the region where women are treated with due regard particularly at the time of marriage. This action of inviting the groom by the bride through an emissary with a request to attend definitely the marriage ceremony formally lowers the status of women. And such an action places the girl in a subservient position.

The bride walking around the groom in the marriage ceremony

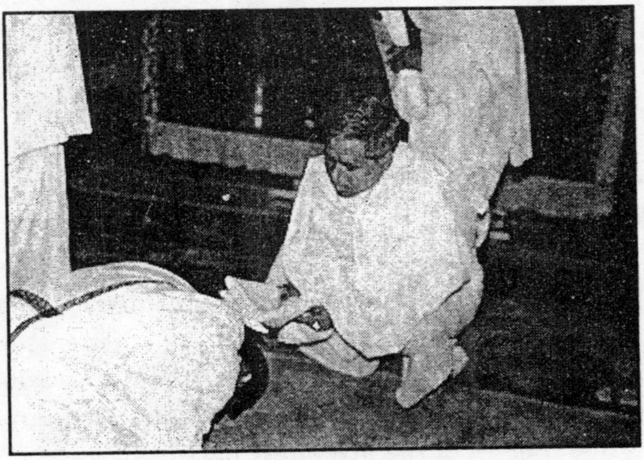

Showering blessing to the groom by the close relatives of the bride after marriage

The Day of Luhongba (Marriage) Ingredients

Sweets and fruits like Kabok (puffed rice), Kwa (betel nut and leaves), banana, cane sugar, etc. are carried by the groom's side. Cloths for offering to the Palas like Khudei (loin cloth), Joypur, etc. are also included in the host of items carried. The amount of 'Kabok' is significantly large and the same is carried by two persons on a large basket known as 'Ningei'. The amount should be such that it should.be able to offer everybody present there.

In the past the marriage ceremony was short and simple. And the same was held in the morning. The ceremony was held in the presence of a few elderly persons of the neighbourhood. There was no decoration at all in and around the scene of marriage ceremony. The dress of both the bride and groom was also very simple. The bride did not wear the dress 'Potloi'. What she wore was a 'Phanek' (undergarment) and an 'Ennafi (a long cloth worn around the body). The act of walking around the groom by the bride and the subsequent showering of flowers by the bride to the groom which is known as 'Lei Chaiba' in the local parlance; was also not practised by the Andros. What was usually done was that both the bride and groom sat together on the 'Luhongphal'. a wooden seat especially prepared for this purpose only. They sat for a while followed by a spell of bowing to the elders attending the ceremony.

The offering of Athenpots by the groom's side to the household deities of the bride's house constitute the ritual aspect of the ceremony. Keeping entact the Athenpots in the secluded areas of the deities, and as a mark of concluding the ceremony the sweets and fruits brought from the groom's house is distributed to the attending persons irrespective of the boy's and girl's side. While the attending persons are busy in enjoying the offered items both the bride and groom perform their customary exercises in the house of the bride. While entering the house the bride is led by a woman of the family. The groom also follow the bride and he is led by a friend or by an 'Arangba' available around there. Both the bride and groom perform a hectic spell of bowing to the elders inside the house. They also pray to the household deities in the house. After accomplishing their customary service inside the house they sit for awhile in the verandah and thus finally parted for the new home of the bride.

Now-a-days a number of additions have been, made to marriage ceremony which make the occasion more ceremonial and festive looking. And the addition can be counted as an influence of the Meiteis. As a result the occasion is becoming more time consuming and less economical; although it is more attractive and festive. At present the groom attend the wedding after a march accompanied by a band party. At the gate of the house he is welcomed by a fire service known as 'Mei-okpa'. Then he sits at his designated place which is traditionally located at the north-eastern corner of the 'Mamang Shangoi' (the front out house). The festival is held in the courtyard with devotional song sung by 'Pala' singers. Cloths are also offered to the Palas. At a certain stage of the ceremony the bride wearing the 'gagra' walks around the groom for a number of times and occasionally showers flowers on the groom. At the fag end of the ceremony a few women goes to a pond and set free a few live 'Ngamus' (a fish) in the water. In this the women also accompany a light in their hand. Finally the bride is carried on a charoit (Dolai) with the same band-party used by the groom. Thus with the above additions a transformation has taken place in the traditional marriage scene. However, the basics of the ceremony, e.g. sitting together by the bride and groom on the 'Luhongphal' and finally a prayer to the household deities remain unchanged by the above transformations.

Chak-Kumba or Chak-Kouba

On the fifth day after marriage a get together between the two families along with some friends and relatives is performed at the residence of the girl's parents. To the Meities this is called as 'Chak Kouba', but the Andros term it as 'Chak-Kumba'. A few friends of the girl as well as for the boy will attend the feast. Elderly persons, a few in number from both the girl' and boy's side will also attend it. No ritual is included in it. This 'Chak-Kumba' is held either before noon or in the evening, depending upon the convenience of the girl's family. Serving fish or vegetable is depended on the wishes of the girl's parents. If they can afford fish, it is upto them. But here a small amount of 'Yu' is accompanied by the boy's parents which is meant for the elderly persons. The sole purpose 'Chak-Kumba' in 'Andro' is to re-introduce the two families so as to re-enforce the newly established relationship. This will bring better understanding and peaceful relationship between the two families. But since the recent past a transformation has taken shape as regard the items carried by the boy's side. In the past the boy's side attended the feast with an empty hand only accompanying a small amount of 'Yu' (liquor). But now-a-days a number of items including sweets (Kabok, etc.), Kwa (betel nuts and leaves), fruits (banana, orange, etc.) are accompanied by the boy's side Besides, they also carry 'Athenpots' prepared out of the vegetables available in the season.

The amount of 'Yu' (liquor) is also increased. What is carried on the day of 'Chak-Kouba' is not less than those carried on the day of 'Haijapot' and 'Waroipot'.

Dan Chak Chaba

A ceremony which immediately perform after 'Mangani Chakouba' or 'Chak-Kumba' is 'Dan Chak Chaba'. This ceremony marks the difference in marriage with that of the Meiteis, however, in the way of social compulsion and participation. In the case of the Meiteis 'Ningol Chak-Kouba' or 'Mangani Chak-Kouba' is the concluding gathering in the long process of marriage. Here in Andro 'Dan Chak Chaba' is the concluding gathering with the inclusion of a feast arranged by the groom's parents. In outward appearance it resembles to reciprocate the 'Mangani Chak-Kouba' organised by brides parents. But this is certainly not the case and one needs to go much deeper into the social organisation of the Andros. Again in 'Dan Chak Chaba' the number of participants shrinks to their close relative only. This is favourably performed on the next day after 'Mangani Chak-Kouba' before occuring death on either side of the two families. This will facilitate in the participation of the close relatives in the funeral service in the event of death of a person from either of the two families. In Andro the participation in funeral service by the relatives is a must as the established custom dictates. So the gathering 'Dan Chak Chaba' provides the opportunity to re-assemble the close relatives of both the involved families thereby facilitating re-introduction among themselves so as to cement their newly established relationship. What is held on the day is almost the same that occured in the day of 'Mangani ChakKouba'. On 'Mangani Chak-Kouba' the procession starts from the groom's side accompanying fruits, sweets and 'Athenpots' for offering to house-hold deities, etc. The reverse is the case in 'Dan Chak Chaba' where the procession starts from the bride's side along with the above items. After their arrival at the groom's house there follows a spell of hectic exchange of bowing on either side of the two relatives. However, the act of paying obeisance is initiated by the bride and groom. The gathering concludes with another spell of bowing; in this case also to be initiated by the newly wed couple; however, after the feast.

Mandop Mapu in Marriage

In Andro there are a few astrologers of their own. So in the event of selecting 'Luhongphal' (an auspicious day) both the families approaches, as a custom, the astrologer'. And the day so find out is make known to the remaining astrologer in the village. This is necessary because 'Luhongphal' cannot be given two in a day. In Andro there cannot be two marriages on a single day. Crises may erupt in the village if there is breach in the custom. So in order to avert such an undesired situation the involved families should make known the selected day to the other astrologers as soon as possible. And as a tradition the astrologer who gave or selected the auspicious day should take part in the marriage. Besides 'Mandop Mapu' also take part in the marriage, 'Mandop Mapu' - the owner or leader of the gathering- his participation in the marriage is essential for the smooth conduct of the ceremony. And no marriage can be held in the absence of 'Mandop Mapu'. There is only one 'Mandop Mapu' in the whole of Andro. And the appointment of such a person is highly selective. The person should posses certain qualities as regard his health, age, wealth and the possibility to spare time in social activities, etc. First he must be the oldest person in the village with a good health. He must also be a person who has least involvement in the domestic works. He spares time when the situation demands his involvement in such ceremonies. The tenure of a 'Mandop Mapu' is three years only. If the person wants to retire during his tenure he will hand over the task to another person. In this case also the person who has to receive the post must be the next oldest person in the village, next to the retiring 'Mandop Mapu'.

Line of Promotion of Mandop Mapu

An oldest person cannot hold the post of 'Mandop Mapu' simply considering his age. He must be an experienced person with an adequate knowledge of handling the customary' rites, rituals and ceremonies. And he must be a person who has involved in many rites, rituals and related ceremonies in the village. And above all this he must be a person who has served the post of 'Puren'. 'Puren' is the leader of 'Arangpham' and 'Ningolcha'. *['Arangpham' are the group of youths* who *are below 40 year of age and* who *works as arrangers in ceremonies and rituals at individual and village level. 'Ningolcha' are the young unmarried girls of the village]*. The tenure of both the 'Puren' and 'Madop Mapu' is three years only. At the completion of three years the 'Mandop Mapu' automatically retires. In such a situation the 'Puren' prepares to step in the important vacant seat. A simple ceremony marks the retirement of the 'Puren' and the same is held at his residence.

It is a simple ceremony of dinning together the 'Yu' (liquor) and 'Shingju' (a traditional raw vegetable Palao). However, the required amount of 'Yu' is prepared by the outgoing and incumbent 'Arangbas'. 'Ninglochas'-the girl's they also contribute a small amount of money, nominally Rs. 5/- or 10/- each. The ceremony is to be attended by the retiring 'Mandop Mapu' and all the seven members of 'Loishang'-the village authority. At the conclusion of the ceremony the retiring 'Mandop Mapu' hands over his equipments to the retiring 'Puren'. Thus the handing over of the equipments (knife, scissor, etc.) marks the promotion of the retiring, 'Puren' to the post of 'Mandop Mapu'.

Shengdokpa

The Andros follow the endogamous community marriage system very strictly. The ceremony 'Shengdokpa' appears when someone from their community marries a girl from other community. This is a ceremony of enrolling a girl of other community to their social set up. 'Shengdokpa'; its literal meaning is to clean. A girl from other community is counted as impure or unclean as the word implied. So this, ceremony clean up the girl and subsequently admitted her to their social order. This is performed with a feast which include 'Yu' (local liquor). It necessarily invites all the seven office-bearers of 'Loishang' - the village authority. Besides the presence of all the 'Pibas' (clan heads:) of all the lineages is also a must. So all the 15 or 16 Pibas are also invited in the ceremony. Basically such a ceremony is the direct outcome of the nature of cremation in Andro. Andro has a peculiar type of cremation which has its root as a social institution in their society. As a custom the cremation in Andro is executed by only two persons. Although a number of persons, close relatives of the deceased and others, follows the dead procession upto crematorium. They will stay there till the necessary customary activities are performed. And they leave the place leaving the task of cremation to the two persons. The two persons are named as 'Maksha' and 'Ningol Matung Enba'. So on this day of 'Shengdokpa' the 'Maksha' and 'Ningol Matung Enba' of the girl are appointed. This is necessary because they are the only two persons who will cremate her in the event of her dead. No other person in the village can execute the cremation. On this day the 'Maksha' and 'Ningol Matung Enba' of the girl are selected from the different lineages. Each lineage has its own 'Maksha' in the manner there are 'Pibas' for the separate lineages. 'Ningol Matung Enba' is a male relative of the girls parents side. It may be her brothers, uncles or other male relatives. In such a case the girl has no such a person as she is from other community. So, the appointment of a 'Ningol Matung Enba' from a lineage of Andro is a necessity. On this day a 'Maksha' from a lineage and a person from another lineage for 'Ningol Matung Enba' are selected. And thus the selection of the above two persons completes the ceremony 'Shengdokpa'.

CHELHONG (ELOPEMENT)

In the 'Chelhong' type of marriage a simple ceremony named 'Loukhatpa' replaces the much bigger 'Luhongba' (marriage) ceremony. The day for 'Loukhatpa' is conveniently fixed by the girl's side. 'Yu', cigars, bidi, Kwa (betel nuts and leaves), fruits and sweets, etc. are carried by the boy's side to the house of girl's parents. The groom is accompanied by a few of his friends. Some elderly persons from their neighbourhood are also invited for the ceremony. The girls parents also invite a selected number of elderly persons from their locality. After a short march the groom arrives at the house of the girl. Now he has to face some customary rigours. He cannot sit on its own nor he cannot proceed to verandah.

He has to remain standing at a designated place in the courtyard along with his friends. The arrangement is such. that the elderly persons of the girl's side remain sitting on the verandah. After a while an elderly person from the boy's side approaches the elderly persons of the girl's side at the verandah and makes a fervent request to allow the boy to climb the verandah so as to enable him to bow to all those present. With a permission from the girl's parents side the boy (groom) ascends the Verandah and bow to all those present on the verandah. Here also he has to remain prostate on the ground for a while till someone from them (elderly persons) touches him on the head. The elderly persons on the verandah assigns someone from among them to do the needful to the lying boy. Persons from boy's side say; 'Loukhatpiro', 'Chanbiro', 'Nungshibiro', to the assigned person. The attending -persons from the boy's side ask the assign person to forgive, to approve and to please the boy. Accordingly the assign person says; 'Loukhatpire' and touches the head of the boy (groom). Thus by such a simple act their marriage is approved by the society. With the conclusion of this act the groom leaves the place. In this manner the 'Chalhong' marriage is accomplished.

Changing Status of Chelhong Marriage

On the day of 'Loukhatpa' for 'Chelhong' marriage the bride is accompanied by the groom, his parents, relatives and friends. Prior to this ceremony she is not allowed to visit her ancestral home. Her parents refuse her presence in her ancestral home as punishment of her breaching the custom of the community. But on this day she who comes with some of her friends in the marriage procession rushes to her parents home with her mother who remain there to receive her. In the past engagement form of marriage was considered the most prestigious form of marriage. And this was true in the Meitei society also. But now-adays such traditional values are gradually disappearing in both the societies. And people in both the societies have started offering the later option, i.e. 'Chelhong'. In fact there are reasons which forces to accept the later option. Time is one factor; people want to save time as number of engagements increases in the modern society both in the individual and social level. Saving of money is another factor. It enables to save a significant amount of money which are expended in the long process of engagement form of marriage. Subsequent to such developments the status of engagement form of marriage and Chelhong is gradually converging.

KEINA KATPA

This kind of marriage can be described as in camera marriage involving a small number of persons. There is no context of ritual. 'Keina Katpa' arises when the bride and groom desire to accomplish the marriage with least publicity and at shortest time. And it seldom happens. One or two elderly persons, desirably their parents, from both the sides are present in the small gathering. There is no need of wearing traditional marriage customs. Wearing of fine clothes is enough. The bride and groom will sit together for a while in presence of the small gathering. They will exchange a garland on their necks to be begun first by the groom. Thus ends the "Keina Katpa' ceremony. All those present in the gathering are the eyewitnesses of the marriage of the boy and girl.

Marriage Laws

The Andros followed a strict exogamous clan marriage system. At the same time they were endogamous in relation to other communities around them. However, a changed environment is visible after the abolition of monarchy and the subsequent introduction of democratic institutions in the state. But still exogamous clan marriage is entact. The change is on the endogamous relationship with other communities. Traditionally the Andro community is grouped together in six (6) Salais (clans) whereas its counterpart the Meiteis are clubbed in seven (7) Salais (clans). The Salais in Andro are (1) Khuman, (2) Ningthouja, (3) Moirang, (4) Kha-Ngamba, (5) Luwang and (6) Angom. The sub-clans or lineages under one Salai (clan) cannot establish marriage relationship among themselves. As an instance the lineages Yumkhaibam, Heikrujam and Leishungbam who are under the clan 'Khuman' cannot establish marriage relationship among themselves. For this they have to approach to other Salals (clans). Likewise the lineages Phanjoubam, Sagolshem, Ningthoujam, Shamchetshabam of Ningthouja Salai; Puthem, Thokchom of Moirang Salai; Chingakham of Kha-Nganba; Hijam, Salam of Luwag Salai and Asheibam, Sarubam, Sarungbam of Angom Salai (clan) cannot inter-marry among themselves. At the stage of Salai (clan) it shows the progenitor of the corresponding lineages. But with the introduction of exogamous clan marriage the Salai is transformed to its synonymous term 'Yek'. 'Yek' literally means enemy implying that the lineages under one 'Salai' has become enemy among themselves the moment they want to establish marriage relationship. In the past such a customary law was strictly imposed in the village. And the one who breached such a custom had to face severe punishment. He was expelled from the village administration, although he was not physically removed from the village. He was removed from the membership of 'Pana' administration.

Consequently he was debarred of the helps and privileges that has to be attained from the communities on different occasions. Andro is a close-knit society and every-piece of occasions are community based. So community involvement is a must for the smooth conduct of any kind of observation or celebration at the family level. This exogamous clan marriage is still intact among the Andros.

ISSUES RELATED WITH MARRIAGE:

Divore

If a couple want to settle their differences through divorce then the appeal is made first to the 'Khullakpa' (Village chief). Then 'Khullakpa' put the matter to the remaining members of the village authority which is known as 'Loishang'-it has seven members including 'Khullakpa'. In such a delicate case utmost care is taken not to resort to the extreme step of divorce. So the authority will pursue both sides to come to an amicable settlement base on the principle of omission and commission of their behaviours. However if the authority fail to bring an amicable settlement then they resort to divorce. And their belongings are divided between them. However, the division is in the movable property only, not in the immovable property. Land is excluded in the division. Articles like clothing, utensils and furniture, etc. are divided. All the grown up children will go to the father's side, only the suckling baby will be left to the mother. The father can receive the baby also when it is three years old. But during the three years the father will provide 12 bags of paddy for the child every year. If there is an agreement between the father and mother the child can stay with the father till he or she is fully grown up.

Dowry

All sorts of items which were necessary in running a new family was included in the dowry. Ginning machine, Lashing Kapon (a basket) and Huitri (an instrument *for* straightening cotton), spinning wheel, loin cloth, utensils, earthen pots, mirror, cupboard, Ngabong (generally above 20 to 30 in number), cloths of different uses including 'Khudei' (loin cloth *for* women), etc. were the items essentially given as dowry. Ngabong (thick cotton cloth) has many uses, so they were given in large numbers. So as a custom a day is fixed ahead of the appointed day for marriage; and on this day the girls from the neighbourhood of the bride used to wash the 'Ngabongs' including the other clothes. But nowadays with the advance of time the items of dowry is also changed. And many modern amenities are included in the dowry. At the same time many traditional items are gradually disappearing from the scene of dowry.

Marriageable Age

Early marriage prevailed in the past. And the popular age was in the later teens. However, these days late marriage is becoming popular and early marriage is gradually disappearing from the scene of marriage.

Levirate, Sororate and Polygamy are not popular behaviour among the Andros. And they do not have social sanction. However, compelled by unavoidable circumstances the above mentioned practices are found in Andro, though in rare cases.

Kingship

Affiliation of lineages on different clans.

A. Khuman Salai (clan)

1. Yumkhaibam
2. Heikrujam
3. Leishungbam

B. Ningthouja Salai

4. Phanjoubam
5. Sagolshem
6. Ningthoujam
7. Shamchetshabam

C. Moirang Salai

8. Puthem
9. Thokchom

D. Kha-Ngamba Salai

10. Chingngakham

E. Luwang Salai

11. Hijam
12. Salam

F. Angom Salai

13. Asheibam
14. Sarubam
15. Sarungbam.

FROM MARRIAGE TO CHILDBIRTH

After marriage the daughter is not left alone. And it is the mother who always gathers information on the changing environment of the daughter. At the same time the mother is kept well-informed of the development occured to her. And so at the advance stage of pregnancy of around ninth (9th) month the daughter is invited for a lunch. On this day the daughter is treated with 'Sareng' fish, a fish which has its name for its delicious taste. Other fishes having smooth skin are also treated.

However, 'Sareng' is more popular. In the tradition of Andro there is not the practice of sending 'Chaphu-Uyan' (cooking pots) to the daughter when she is in the advance stage of pregnancy. Although the practice, under the influence of the Meities, has appeared among the Andros in small numbers. However, the tradition is alive among the Meiteis. The cooking pots known as 'Chaphu-Uyan' are sent along with dry fish, 'Meitei Thum' (local salt) and chips of pine, etc. to the daughter. However, the lids of pots are excluded on the very day. The lids are brought on the day of 'Epan' of the baby', 'Epan' - the birth ceremony.

REFERENCES

1. Oral interview with S. Kullachandra and S. Lalito of Andro Khunou Leikai.
2. Oral interview with Y. Dharmo Singh of Andro Awang Leikai.
3. Oral interview with S. Thambal.
4. Oral interview with N. Shyam.
5. Oral interview with Chingakham Thambal on 16.03.06.

6

BELIEFS AND PRACTICES AROUND DEATH CEREMONY AND PHILOI - THE LAST RITE

There are opposing views on the ways of disposal of death in the past in Andro. Cremation is known to the Andros since the ancient past as found mentioned from the literature "Poireiton Khunthokpa". However, some scholars are of the view that the incident of 'Poireiton Khunthokpa' is related to the occasion of unnatural deaths like drowning, hanging etc. They are of the view that in the past the Andros also buried the deaths in the ground putting the bones in an earthen jar. But no one can claim the age of adopting cremation in Andro. Again the practice of burying a piece of burnt bone in an earthen jar known as 'Luphu' which was once practised in Andro is a testimony of cremation in the past. In addition the practice of burning rice on an earthen plate (Kambi) beginning from 'Mang' (crematorium) to the house of the deceased till the day of death ceremony cannot be a tradition which may develop in the 18th century, i.e. after the adoption of Hinduism in Manipur. However, transformations have appeared in small scale in the procedure of disposal of death by burning which is in current in Andro. The same can be apprehended in the discussion to be taken up in the following manner.

DISPOSAL OF DEATH

On the dying moment of a person a ' Maiba' (priest) takes care of the dying man or woman. At the critical stage the 'Maiba' gives his hint to pay the last respect to the dying person by the close relatives including father, mother, son, daughter, brother, sister etc. The dying person is kept inside the house till death at 'Phammang' the space in front of his or her bed,' Meanwhile a 'Shang' (small hut) is prepared at 'Khangenpham'- south-eastern side of the courtyard. The 'Shang' is the resting place of the death person till it is ready to carry to crematorium. At the last moment the dying person is carried out of the house through 'Naktha'- (which is also known as Ashithong) - the left side of the verandah. This practice is based on the belief that the soul of a dying person leaves the house through this side of the verandah.

The dying person is carried around the hut for three times in anticlockwise direction which is known as "Shang-Koiba". And finally the body is placed inside the hut. At this stage.the 'Maiba' leaves the dying person as a mark of declaring the death of the person. But while placing the body it is placed above a 'La Laton'- the end part of banana leaf.

The head is kept rest on a 'Laphu Makak Tangkhai'- (half of a piece of banana stem). Afterawhile the corpse is carried out of the 'Shang' to the either side of the house (yennakha) for a brief bath. The corpse is now dressed with new cloths including headgear for man, khudei (loin cloth) and long cloth. For women she is dressed with a 'Pungou Phanek' (undergarment) and 'Ennaphi' (long cloth). If she is a married women a belt (traditional) is also included around her waist. Again after dressing the body is carried inside the 'Shang', the hut. When all these are taking place a group of persons prepare the 'Ku' (coffin). Long cloths (Feijup, Maitha) for sleeping is placed in the coffin along with a small pillow. The body is placed above the cloths in the coffin. The coffin is strengthened with a binding by 'Paya'- bamboo chips. A simple drawing is made on the coffin by using ginger (Yaingang), charcoal and lime. A drawing of 'Kairen Kaichao' is also included in the coffin. Last of all a fine cloth covers the coffin.

LAI TANBA

A tradition which is no longer in practice is the 'Lai Tanba' by the dead body. This is an act of warding off 'Lai'- the spirit by the corpse.

This is performed only when the death person is dressed up after taking bath. In fact this is an act of shooting arrow to the 'Lai' with the help of somebody. While shooting he also shouts. This was a practice for man only, not for woman.

While the corpse is in 'Khangenpham' the message is related to the locality. And this is the duty of 'Shingjuba' (Shinshuba) of the 'Leikai'. Every 'Leikai' (local) has 'Shinglup' (organisation for firewood) and each 'Shinglup' has one 'Shingjuba'.

According to Yumkhaibam Dharmo Singh, former 'Khullkpa' of Andro, there was hearsay of putting the coffin inside the house. But he is not certain of the hearsay as he did not physically experience it.

When the corpse is in the coffin a ball made (fibul) of 'Ngabong' cloth is passed for three times above the coffin with the words "Nayama Ngaiba, Ebong Ngaiba, Fibul Leina Thana Oinabiyo". Next a coil is made of 'Nahong' (a cloth used to fasten a baby on the back of a person) and is placed on the forehead of the corpse. Now the 'Fibul' (a ball made of cloth) is laid to rest *on* the coil of 'Nahong'. Thus the corpse is now ready to be carried to crematorium.

In the past cremation was carried out at many places according to the wishes of the family. Cremation in one's homestead was also in vogue. There were crematoriums for particular lineages and still some of it is available. However, due to increasing land pressure crematorium for the community is increasingly popular. Since the ancient days the coffin is carried to crematorium with a procession. However, a transformation is visible in the component of the procession. In the past the coffin was carried with the accompaniment of flute, drum, 'Pena' (a string instrument), 'Khou Shaba' (a ritual dance with spear) and 'Shuk Khokpa'. In the past the 'Pena' was sung in 'Chakpa' dialect but now-adays it is replaced by Manipuri. 'Khou Shaba' (ritual dance with spear) was included as a mark of respect to revered persons like 'Khullakpa' (village chief) and octogenarian persons.

'Khou-Shaba' lead the procession and followed by the drums. However, all these act cease to perform when they reach the crematorium. In the procession the 'Maksha' and 'Ningol Matung Enba' the two persons who ultimately will carry out the cremation is compulsorily included. The 'Maksha-Manglen' wears a 'Yempak' - a traditional umbrella made of straw or bark of bamboo. The 'Maksha' and 'Ningol Matung Enba' carry 'Lang Ahingba' (sacred thread) on the way, and leaves pieces of it at intervals *on* their journey to crematorium. *"Shuk Ahumna Pheithinnaraga Shorok Yangbithakta Kaidang Kaidang Pugani"* - the coffin is carried resting *on* three 'Shuks' (mortar used in rice pounding) with a graceful movement. Another item which is last but not the. least is to carry all the bed, sheets, pillow and clothes used during illness. An abandoned practice at the crematorium is to shoot at the firewood piled up to rest the coffin. Shooting the piled firewood by an arrow with the help of a 'Shairong' (catapult) is done before it is burnt. Now this practice is extinct along with the different musical instruments accompanied in the procession. The only instrument withstanding the change is the flute. Drum (Pung) is also no longer in use. Even the use of flute is depended on the availability of the flute singer. Another change is in the use of cloth covering the coffin. In the past it was a custom to use a fine cloth. But now a days it is replaced by an ordinary cloth. According to Ch. Thambal the practice to cover the coffin by a cloth is simply an act of hiding the ugly appearance of the corpse.

The carrying of the coffin is the activity of the community or 'Leikai' (local). However, at the crematorium everything has become the activity of the close relatives and the two persons 'Maksha' and 'Ningol Mutung Enba'. The other persons who were in the procession has become audience of the occasion. According to Ph. Modon of 'Andro Kharam Leikai' the lighting of funeral pyre is done by Maksha' and 'Ningol Matung Enba'. However, Y. Dharmo of Andro Awang Leikai is of the opinion that it is the 'Ningol Matung Enba' who lights the pyre. When the fire start razing the ritual 'Mei Koiba' is performed. It is an act of going around the burning pyre with a 'Pun' (earthen pitcher) full of water. The carrier of the 'Pun' with full of water is the closest relative of the deceased. But other close relatives will also take part in the 'Mei Koiba'. Unlike the 'Meities' the person with the 'Pun' do not carry a burning stick in the act of going around the burning pyre. The person with the 'Pun' with full of water and along with the close relatives of the decease goes around the burning pyre for a number of times in the clockwise direction. The carrier of the 'Pun' is deliberately a male, a woman cannot do it. According to Ph. Modon of Kharam Leikai the act of going around the fire is held for five times for male and six times for female depending upon the sex of the deceased. While walking around the burning pyre water is poured from the 'Pun' at the four corners of the pyre where a wooden post is fixed to the ground at each corner. But while pouring water the person bends backward and pour it from the back. But he cannot look at the back. Water is also poured in the small pot hole made on the head side of the pyre. The person who has to carry the 'Pun' should take a bath before doing this. The ending of 'Mei Koiba' marks a stage of cremation). At this stage all the persons, except 'Maksha' and 'Ningol Matung Enba', leave the crematorium, Now it has become the task of the two assigned persons to reduce everything present in the pyre to ashes. There are 'Pibas' (head of a lineage) of every lineage, so also there are 'Maksha' of every lineage. But he will do the work of other lineages. He is in charge of one or more lineages, whereas 'Ningol Matung Enba' is the male maternal relatives of the deceased person. Following is a list of 'Maksha' of different 15 lineages of Andro.

1. 'Maksha' of Chingakham is Yumkhaibam
2. 'Maksha' of Heikrujam is Sharungbam
3. 'Maksha' of Sarubam is Salam
4. 'Maksha' of Yumkhaibam is Puthem
5. 'Maksha' of Salam is Phanjoubam
6. 'Maksha' of Puthem is Chingakham
7. 'Maksha' of Phanjoubam is Chingakham
8. 'Maksha' of Hijam is Phanjoubam
9. 'Maksha of Ningthoujam is Puthem
10. 'Maksha' of Sharungbam is Yumkhaibam
11. 'Maksha' of Shagolshem is Hijam
12. 'Maksha' of Thokchom is Asheibam
13. 'Maksha' of Asheibam is Ningthoujam
14. 'Maksha' of Khunnumayum is Chingakham
15. 'Maksha' of Shamchetshabam is Chingakham

AN EXTINCT TRADITION OF LUPHU

Here 'Lu' is bone and 'Phu' is earthen pitcher; so 'Luphu' means an earthen pitcher meant for keeping a piece of bone. There was a tradition of burying an earthen pitcher known as 'Luphu' in the ground in the crematorium containing a piece of burnt bone. For this a woman along with some persons goes to the crematorium at a time when the cremation is about to over. The woman, preferably the daughter of the deceased, carries an ordinary pitcher on her back by a special cloth named 'Nahongphi' a designed one. If the person has no daughter, then a daughter of his or her lineage will carry out the job. When the cremation is over the fire is carefully extinguished and creates an environment to collect the bone. For this a forceps is made out of 'Meihanchei'- the bamboo stick used in burning the corpse. The burnt bone cannot be collected by hand. So the bamboo 'Chegap' (forceps) collect the piece of burnt bone in the earthen pitcher. Here the collection is done by the assigned woman. The piece of burnt bone so collected is brought home on the back of the woman. The piece of bone is washed thoroughly by water and followed by 'Yu' (liquor).

Now the piece of bone is put inside a 'Luphu'- a well decorated tripod. The tripod is enveloped by threads of red, green and black which is woven around it. In addition to the piece of bone gold, silver, utensils and cloths, etc. are the items shared to the deserted soul. A 'Luphu' containing all the above items is now covered by a lid made of mud known as 'Kambi' (an earthen plate). Now the decorated 'Luphu' containing the washed bone is carried to the crematorium again on the back of another woman. The same woman cannot do the task of collecting and carrying of the 'Luphu' to the crematorium again. But the carrying of the 'Luphu' to the crematorium is performed with much fanfare to the tune of flute, Pena (a stringed instrument), drum and dish. Burying is *done* near the Mang (crematorium) with the accompaniment of the above instruments. But while burying the 'Luphu' is put inside a big 'Kharung' - a big earthen jar. This 'Luphu' is buried on the day of cremation. Now it is a death practice and only a few elder persons remembers it. For the younger generation it is completely foreign to them. Cremating in one's homestead is also gone along with the tradition of 'Luphu'. Again maintaining crematorium for the different lineages was also a tradition. So the charcoal was piled up in huge heaps for the separate lineages. A person from another lineage could not touch it, and could not use it for burning. If anybody acts against the custom he was bound to face punishment. He will be fined according to the custom of the community known as 'Wakongba'. But now-a-days this is also no more visible.

GANGOU YANBA

This is also a tradition which is no more continued. Two posts of 'Upan' tree is fixed to the ground. And above it rests another branch of the same tree so as to hang something on it. Now five cut out pieces of 'Yengdou' (a small bamboo like plant) is coiled unevenly by the flesh of banana plant. The same is burnt in the fire so as to leave burning marks on the 'Yengdou'. When the banana flesh is uncoiled after the burning it leaves marks which produces an assorted colour of black and white which is known as 'Marang-Marangba' in the local parlance. Such a prepared 'Gang' is hanged on the branch of 'Upan' tree resting on the two posts. And the 'Gang' is five in number. The belief goes that the five 'Gang' represents the five souls. In the words of Ph. Modon of Andro Kharam Leikai "Gang Yanba" was a practice which was held in the event of death of a male person not in the death of a bachelor. 'Gang Yanba' was performed for old persons, a dignitary in Pana office, a married person and for a person who has promoted to the office of 'Loisang'. Women and children were excluded from such a practice.

The tradition of burying a piece of burnt bone, the act of shooting the funeral pyre by an arrow with the help of a catapult and finally the hanging of 'Gang' has disappeared from the village. In the past all these made the funeral service a time consuming activity. In contrast to it now the process is considerably shortened. In the meantime the act 'Lai- Tanba' is also not in sight. What is really practised in these days is that a majority of persons takes part in the funeral procession as well as in the cremation. However, a few persons remain in the house of the deceased person who engage in cleaning the house. All these are executed under the command of an elderly person known as 'Shinshuba'. However, very old persons are excluded from such activities. Persons who are of the same age with 'Shinshuba' or younger to him has to obey his command. The elders who has taken part in the cremation returns to their respective houses for a brief bath. Further they will assemble again at the house of the deceased person, but this time with washed cloths known as 'Fisheng'. The elders will go in a hog with flowers to the crematorium for offering. Meanwhile the two persons; 'Maksha' and 'Ningol Matung Enba' makes the necessary environment for the offering by levelling the ground. Fruits (in three shares), betel nuts and leaves (in three shares) and three wax lights is offered at head side and leg side of the Mang (crematorium). Thus the showering of flowers in the 'Mang' ends the funeral service of the deceased person.

DISPOSAL OF DEATH BABY

A baby, both male and female, which has crossed three months of age is cremated. And a baby under three months of age is treated as 'Shoiren'. And for them a different way of disposal is performed. They are not cremated but they are buried in the ground. The baby to be disposed is kept inside a jar. For an easy access of the baby the neck of the jar is removed carefully. The baby is kept above three 'Maitha' (long cloth) and three 'Theijup' (Feijup) (quilt like cloth) which is put one above the other. A few pulses which are fried to black; may be peas, soyabeans or 'Chakhawai' are put inside the jar, some four or five pebbles are also put in the jar. And this is the brief ritual which is based on the belief that the soul of the baby is allowed to return to the family only when the pebbles germinates or the fried pulses germinates.

But this is an indirect treatment to the soul not to return to the family again. The objective of the treatment to the soul is not to repeat such unwanted death to the family in future. Now the jar containing the baby is covered by another jar. But the burial of the jar can not be done in the vicinity of the village; one has to execute it on the yonder side of the river where there is no population. Burying in the vicinity of the village is not treated as a good practice as the belief says that it may bring misfortune to the locality.

DEATH CEREMONY IN ANDRO

The death ceremony is held on the fifth day for male and on the sixth day for female, from the death of the person. Although the final ritual is held on the 5th or 6th day of the death of the person, but a beginning is made since the day of cremation. Since the day of cremation the 'Miren Polang' - a basket like structure made of bamboo strips is hanged near the verandah side of the front door. A day before the death ceremony meals are offered to the 'Miren Polang'. And the same is also offered on the day of death ceremony. However, the ritual begins at the depth of night on the day of cremation. A person will go to the 'Mang' (crematorium) at the depth of night along with a small amount of black rice, prawn (khajing) and 'ngakha' (a small kind of fry) putting on a 'Kambi' (earthen plate). Going to crematorium at the depth of night is fearsome and so a courageous person is needed for the purpose. The black rice is burnt at the 'Mang' and he steps towards home fanning the burning rice. But he will stop at a place after a short march leaving the burning rice and others items as a mark that he ends his march for the night. Since the next day the march is held in the day time. And on the second day also he stops after a short walk by burning the same items. And the march continues till the day before the day of death ceremony. On this day the igniting of black rice is held at the gate of the deceased.

On the day of death ceremony the igniting of black rice is done by the women of the family at the inner side of the front door. It is the day of consecrating the house which is considered that the house has been desecrated on the death of the person. On this day of death ceremony the 'Miren-Polang' is dressed according to the sex of the deceased person. If the deceased is a male then the 'Miren-Polang' is dressed male customs. Again if the deceased is a female then the same is dressed female customs.

The tradition of 'Miren-Polang' and igniting of black rice is closely associated with the belief in soul. In a sense the tradition is a reflection that soul do not depart the body and the family immediately after the death of the person. And the belief continues that the soul stays somewhere around the 'Mang' (crematorium) after cremation of the person. But there arises the need to accommodate the soul to proper place and finally to release the soul to its heavenly place. Here 'Miren Polang' is the assumed house of the soul. In fact this 'Polang' is the embodiment of human skeleton, i.e. the body. Again 'Miren' or 'Thawai Miren' is the soul and 'Polang' or 'Hakchang Polang' is the skeleton in the local parlance. So 'Miren-Polang' signifies the skeleton of the soul. The igniting of black rice is the act of persuading the soul to return to the house. So the soul is persuaded by the person with the burning rice to return to the house after a march covering more than four or five days. On the day of death ceremony the igniting of black rice is performed at the inner side of the front door near the 'Miren-Polang'. At this stage what is assumed is that the soul at last has agreed to the persuasion and now housed in the 'Miren-Polang'.

Offering made at the crematorium on the day of 'Phiori.'

The ritual performed on the death ceremony is a simple one. For this a well-prepared meal is offered near the 'Urep'- the main pillar in three places. 'Urep' is considered as the secluded place of 'Atiya Guru Shidaba'- the Almighty. In addition to this women of the family burns black rice along with 'Ngakha-Khajing'- the small fry including prawn. The fanning of the burnt black rice is done near the inner side of the front door. A meal is also offered to the 'Miren-Polang'. When all this is done a feast is offered to all those present in the occasion as a service for their sharing of the hardships faced by the family. After the feast the 'Miren-Polang' is carried along with the 'Luklen'(offered meal at the 'Mang' (crematorium). The 'Miren-Polang' is burnt down at the 'Mang'. The 'Luklen' is relished by the accompanying children of the neighbourhood.

PHIROI

Phiroi, which is considered as the last rite of the deceased is held on the first death anniversary. For this a 'Miren-Polang' is necessarily included. A feast is served in this ritual also. The main part of the ritual is story-telling basically the genealogy of the lineage. When this story-telling is undergoing the 'Miren-Polang' is carried to the 'Mang' (crematorium) along with a host of items which are offered as a share of the departed soul. It includes a well-prepared ,meal containing chicken, pork, fish, boiled egg and boiled arum, cane sugar, fruits, flowers, betel-nuts and leaves and a 'Shingju' is also included in the offering. A small amount of rice bear is also included. Clothes for the soul depending upon the sex of the deceased is also offered along with a necklace. A necklace is common for both the sexes. Cloth for male is 'Khaja-Feijom' - dhoti like undergarment and 'Fanek' for female. In addition to this, for male, a 'Lugun' (a sacred thread) is also offered. The offering of clothes may be counted as an act of setting free the soul. Now the soul can go anywhere it like by wearing the clothes. They are given the chance to reborn as a living being. When the offering is over the meal is shared by the accompanying children of the locality. However, children belonging to the same lineage with the deceased cannot eat the meal. The clothes are also given to the children. The 'Lugun' (sacred thread) is given to an elderly person of another lineage other than the lineage of the deceased. At the fag end everything including the 'Miren-Polang' is burnt down and reduced to cinders. The party who executed the offering at the 'Mang' return immediately signalling that the feast may be served to all present in the ceremony. Thus the feast is served only after burning down the 'Miren-Polang'.

1. A girl (below puberty) spinning 'Lang Ahingba."
2. Mondum Polang. (A small basket)
3. 'Lang Ahingba' (thread) is coiled around the bar.
4. Piba of the lineage..
5. Chengbum Ahum (three small heaps of rice).
6. Lainingthou Lairemma placed on winnower.
7. Mangtaruk (a basket)
8. Eratphu (a pitcher)
9. Maiba (priest)
10. Nahaiphu (a pitcher)
11. Phoudang Phou (a basket containing paddy)
12. Khongkan yen (a chicken)
13. Chinphu yen (a chicken)
14. Kharung (a jar containing water)
15. Yangkok (a winnower containing Shingju and Yelhan)
16. A huge heap of rice decorated with branches, leaves, flowers and eggs.
17. Nine small heaps of rice; twelves paris of Chaphu and Uyan placed on banana leaves.

CHUPSA MOITHEMBA

It is another form of death ceremony. And this form of death ceremony is held to unnatural deaths like suicide, drowning and death by lightning, etc. The main theme of the ritual is not to repeat such unwanted unnatural deaths to the family. The ritual is a time-consuming one involving a huge amount of offerings. However, the occasion is very rare. The main part of the ritual is held in the courtyard, however, a beginning is made in the verandah. What is discussed in this text is mainly the various ingredient of the ritual and the positions of the different items in the courtyard including those of the 'Maiba' (priest) and 'Piba' (head of lineage). The chanting of sacred words (Mantra is deliberately excluded from the text as such sacred words are not disclosed to a scholar but to a 'Maiba' (priest) only.

In the past when there was a small population the ritual' Chupsha Moithemba' was executed by a priest of the 'Sana Konung' - the palace. But with the increase in population the pressure on the 'Maiba' also increase. So the palace offered its permission to execute the ritual by a priest of a specified area. By an edict of the 'Sana Konung' the eastern side also got its permission to held the ritual by a priest of the side.

Subsequently the Andro has also conducted the ritual by a priest of its community. For the sake of convenience the position of the different items included and the persons involved in the ritual are arranged in the following manner.

1. A Young Girl (Below Puberty)

A young girl (below puberty) also takes part in the ritual. Her place is at 'Naktha' - the left side of the verandah of the house who is facing the east. According to the belief of this place this 'Naktha' is treated as the passage of death. And as such is the belief a dying person is carried out at this side.

The role of this girl is to produce 'Lang Ahingba' - raw thread for use in the ritual. She has to produce the thread from a single rolled cotton. Even in the event of a break she cannot change to a new rolled cotton. She has to work from the same rolled cotton. The thread so produced is handed over to the 'Maiba' (priest) who in turn place it over a small bamboo pole known as 'Poura'. The ritual begins only when the girl produces the 'Lang-Ahingba' (the sacred thread).

2. Moudum Polang

It is a small bamboo basket made woven by 'Paya' (bamboo strips). It is like the basket used in carrying chickens which is entrapped in it. This 'Polang' is hanged on the 'Naktha' side or left side of the verandah. A small stem of 'Shingnang' is fixed to the eaves-dropper of the 'Naktha' side and on it the 'Polang' is hang or fixed. The items put in the 'Polang' are a small amount of rice, an egg, a hand of banana of odd number and a small amount of puffed rice. This is the share of the 'Maiba', (priest). After performing the ritual the 'Maiba' leaves the house through the gate. At this moment a person from the family shouts 'Maiba'; 'you have forgotten your belongings'. He cannot turn back. The person will hand over the 'Mondum Polang' to the 'Maiba' from the back with the words, "Nacha Khuthek" and the 'Maiba' receives it from his back with the words 'Namou Kati'.

3. Lang Ahingba and Poura

The 'Lang Ahingba' (the sacred thread) is coiled around a small bamboo bar known as 'Poura'. Two small branches of 'Khok-U' tree having joints of about one foot in height is fixed to the ground. Over this a short bamboo bar of around one and a half foot in length is placed. This bamboo bar, known as 'Poura' is made from 'Khokwa' bamboo. A small 'Poura' is favourably selected so as to facilitate in cutting it along with the thread at one stroke of the dagger. Such a 'Poura' is placed just at the edge of the verandah at its 'Naktha' side.

4. Pibagi Phampham

The place of 'Piba' (head of a lineage) is in front of the 'Poura'. But it moves a little to the east. The 'Piba' sits on a 'Lafut'. This 'Lafut' is a seat made of thatch which is coiled into a ring. This is bound by a single 'Paya' (bamboo strip). The 'Piba' sits facing east and places his feet on coin, iron piece and a knife known as 'Khunet Shen', 'Khunet Yot' and 'Khunet Thang'. 'Piba' here is the representation of 'Lainingthou Sanamahi', the principal deity of the Meiteis. His feet is covered by a cloth known as 'Khongkhum-phi' and his back by another cloth known as 'Namphi'. He also wears as headgear. He wears a shirt known as 'Kha-onphi'. The above two items (headgear, Kha-on) are his own. But 'Khongkhum Phi' and Namphi' are given by the house.

5. Chengbum Ahum (Three Small Heaps of Rice)

Just in front of the Piba three small heaps of rice are placed on banana leaves. On each of the heap an egg is placed. A hand of banana of odd number is placed on each of the heap. The heap to the left of the 'Piba' is meant for the 'Maiba' (priest). The heap to the right of the 'Piba' is meant for the 'Piba'. The heap in the middle is meant for the host. But his share can be given to the 'Maiba' if he desires to do so.

6. Lainingthou and Lairemma

A mat made of bamboo strips in the shape of a Humai' (a winnower used in fanning paddy in the field in harvesting) is placed just in front of the 'Cheng bum Ahum'. A broad cloth is placed above the mat. On the right side of it a 'Feijom (dhoti) and a 'Kokyet' (headgear) are placed for 'Lainingthou' - the principal household deity. And on the left side of it a 'Tonga Fanek' (a small undergarment for women) and an Ennafi' (a long cloth) are placed for 'Lairemma' (the goddess).

7. Mangtaruk (A Basket)

A little to the north-east of the seat of 'Lainingthou' and 'Lairemma' a basket known as 'Mangtaruk' is placed. Rice is poured to its brim to the basket. Some eggs are placed above the rice. A hand of banana of odd number is placed above the rice. The basket is covered by a black cloth stitched on its breadth.

8. Eratphu

On the south eastern side of the 'Lainingthou' and 'Lairemma' a pitcher known as 'Eratphu' is placed. This pitcher is involved in the process of the ritual. A small amount of water is stored in it. Inside a betel nut and a piece of banana is dropped.

9. Maiba

The 'Maiba' (priest) sits to the south of the courtyard in line with 'Mangtaruk'. He also sits on a 'Lafut'.

10. Nahaiphu

A little to the north-east of the 'Maiba' another pitcher known as 'Nahaiphu' is placed. The water inside it is treated as holy water. And the same is used in ritual cleaning with 'Tairen' and 'Pungphai'.

11. Phoudang Phou

This basket is placed in front of 'Eratphu'. And this is almost in the same line with 'Nahaiphu'. This basket is filled with paddy to its brim. Above the paddy a garland of small fry, a pair of salt (Meitei thum - local salt) and pair of coin are placed. A small rope, made of jute is tied at the edge of the basket. At the fag end of the ritual the 'Maiba' cut it with a knife. This action is based on the belief that the practice dispels the evil spirit from the house.

12. Khongkan Yen (A Chicken to be Stepped Over)

The place of this 'Khongkan Yen' is a little to the south-east of the 'Maiba'. A chicken *is* kept binding on a small post fixed to the ground. At a certain stage of the ritual the Maiba advise the Piba to step over the chicken and hence the name 'Khongkan Yen'. Here 'Khong' is leg, 'kan' is to step over and 'Yen is chicken.

13. Chiphu Yen (A Chicken to be Blown by Mouth)

A little to the front of 'Khongkan Yen' another chicken known as 'Chinphu Yen' is bound in the above manner as in the case of 'Khongkan Yen'. Again at another stage of the ritual the 'Maiba' advise the 'Piba' to perform 'Chinphuba' and says 'Piba Chinphuro'. Accordingly the 'Piba' collects a mouthful of water from a jar put nearby the chicken. Before this he steps over the Khongkan Yen'. Now the 'Piba' blows the Chinphu Yen' (the chicken) with the water in his mouth. Then other males attending the ritual follow the 'Piba' in blowing the chicken with the water from the jar. However, the 'Piba' does this for three times with the eating of 'Shingju' at intervals. Before taking water from the jar he put a few coins in the jar. However, the blowing is done only once by other males attending the ritual. If the attending males are large in number the chicken sometimes dies by the blowing.

14. Kharung or Chinphu Chaphu (A Jar)

This jar is placed a little to the south-east of the 'Chinphu Yen'. This jar is filled with clean water. As the water is meant for performing 'Chinphuba' and hence it is known as 'Chinphu Chaphu'.

15. Yangkok (A Winnower Oval in Shape)

The 'Yangkok' is placed a little to the north-east of the 'Chinphu Yen'. However, this is a little to the west of the jar. On a side of the 'Yangkok' the 'Yelhan' is kept. 'Yelhan' is the leaf of an unedible plant which is included in the ritual. Once a plant is included in the ritual the plant becomes food taboo for the involving lineage. Such a tradition is still very much alive in Manipur. If a plant is included in such a ritual in any corner of Manipur then it is let known to the remaining members of the lineage with the help of local newspapers. It is make known to the members of the lineage settled in various parts of Manipur that the plant cannot be eaten, it has turn into 'Yelhan'. However, for the Andro's such a publicity is not necessary as most of the male members of the lineage are attending the ritual.

On the other side of the 'Yangkok' the 'Shingju' (raw vegetable palao) of 'Ngamu Phumlou' (a fish) of three or seven in number, 'Heimang Mana' (Heimang leaves) and ginger is placed alongside the 'Yelhan'. Salt and pepper is added so as to make it palatable. This 'Shingju' is used by the 'Piba' when he perform the act of 'Chinphuba' to the 'Chinphu Yen'.

16. Cheng Mapei (Rice Hill)

This rice hill is placed to the front of all the items displayed for the ritual. This is stored on a mat made of bamboo chips known as 'Phaklong'. Rice is stored to a height of around two to three ft. from the ground. Eggs are put over the rice in large numbers exceeding a hundred. All the eggs contributed by the attending persons of the locality are put over the rice hill. Besides, the rice hill is decorated with flowers, branches, twigs and 'Langthrei' plant, etc. so as to look like a hill. In fact this is the representation of 'Nongmaiching' hill.

17. Cheng-Gi Chingshang Napom Mapan (Nine Ranges of Rice)

This nine ranges of rice is placed on the northern side or left side of the courtyard. For this very small pitchers of 24 in number are required. Twelve pairs are made out of the 24 small pitchers. These pitchers are so small that it has no other uses except in the ritual matter. In the pair one pitcher is 'Chaphu' (meant for cooking rice) and the other is Uyan (meant for cooking curry). Small amount of rice is put in the 12 'Chaphu' and small amount of pepper and salt is put in the other 12 'Uyans'. This pairs of pitchers (Chaphu and Uyan) are placed on the right side of a long banana leaf. On the left side of the banana leaf nine ranges of rice is made out of a row of rice spread over the leaf. Rice is poured over the banana leaf in a row and out of this nine pieces are cut so as to represent the nine ranges. Over the nine ranges of rice eggs, branches, twigs, flowers and 'Langthrei' etc. are decorated like in the manner of 'Cheng Mapei'. This is in representation of the nine ranges of 'Nongmaiching' Hill.

As mentioned earlier the text produced here is mainly the various ingredients of the ritual and the positions of the different items including those of 'Piba' and 'Maiba'. The sacred words or language of the ritual is strictly censored and hence sequence of the ritual is kept unexplained. However, all these may be divulge 'to a novice 'Maiba'. But from the above scattered information we can sum up a brief account of the beginning and ending of the ritual. The ritual cannot make a start even when all the relevant items are displaced and placed in their respective positions. The ritual can be kick off only when the girl produces Lang Ahingba' (the sacred thread).

At a certain stage the 'Maiba' says - 'Piba' 'Chinphuro'. Then the 'Piba' step over the 'Khongkan Yen' and proceeds to the 'Kharung' (Jar). There he drops a coin and collects a mouthful of water from the jar. Then he blows the water to the 'Chinphu Yen'. He eats a small amount of 'Shingju' from the Yangkok' (winnower) and blows the chicken with the water from the jar. And he repeats the act for thrice. Again at another stage following the direction of 'Maiba' the 'Piba' chop off the sacred thread coiled on the 'Poura' - the small bamboo bar. The ritual comes to an end only when the jute thread bound on the edge of the basket containing the paddy in the 'Phoudang Phou' is cut by the 'Maiba' with a knife. At the last moment the 'Maiba' collects the 'Mondum Polang' from his back with the word 'Namou Kati'. From the above discussion it is quite clear that it is a ritual which gives more stress on not to repeat such an unnatural death in the family.

Such a ritual cannot be held inside the house. But the inclusion of the principal deity is a necessity. In this context the inclusion of 'Piba' representing the principal deity 'Sanamahi' may be treated as an indirect way of participating the deity in the ritual. An interesting observation is the inclusion of 'Nongmaiching' hill in the ritual, however, modeled by a rice hill and 9 rice ranges. The inclusion of the hill in the ritual modeled by rice and decorated with flowers, twigs, etc. is a form of worshipping the nature. It shows the close relationship of the life of mankind with the nature.

REFERENCES

1. M.S. - Poireiton Khunthokpa.
2. Oral interview with Y. Dharmo Singh former Khullakpa of Andro.
3. Oral interview with the Ph. Modon of Andro Kharam Leikai.
4. Oral interview with Ch. Thambal of Andro Awang Leikai.

BELIEFS AND PRACTICES

A set of beliefs are found mingled in the personal life of the Andros. Such beliefs and practices are mostly similar with that of the Meities, however; there are many which has local colour. Such beliefs, to some extent, influences the life of the Andros thereby regulating their actions. The following is an attempt on such beliefs and practices of the Andros.

1. It is considered inauspicious walking under a 'Polangkhok'a bamboo pole used for drying cloth. So one avoids walking under it.
2. It is also treated inauspicious if one faces a broom early in the morning immediately after leaving his or her bed.
3. A cat crossing the road when one comes out for a mission is counted as a bed omen.
4. The belief of this land treats 'Naktha'- the left side of Verandah as 'Ashithong'- the passage of death. So leaving the house for a mission on the 'Naktha' side of Verandah is considered inauspicious.
5. In the tradition of this land the house itself is a temple, a secluded place for worshipping. So every part of a traditional house has its name. 'Houdong Chakthapham' is also one of them. It is a reserved place for feeding a cat. A cat cannot be fed at another place. It is located in the

'Chakshang'-(kitchen) part of a house. And it is just near a post. It is considered inauspicious if one stands inclining to the post. Further it is believed that the person will become a slave if he or she does incline to the post.

6. In a traditional house there are two main doors the one in the front is known as 'Emangthong' in the traditional parlance. However, in the modern version the one in the front is known as 'Mamangthong'. The custom of this land says that the person should leave the house to the door that the person enters. Entering in the front door and leaving in the back door is not allowed. This custom is very much alive and the elders keeps much attention on it. They will train the younger generation.

7. The Andro's do not use the goat as food. Again they do not keep it in their homes. They do not domesticate it.

8. Pottery is a very old craft in Andro. And it is still flourishing. But this craft is reserved for womenfolk of Andro. Men do not take part in pottery. But here in this craft a 'Leishabi;- an unmarried woman is not allowed to take part in pottery. She can do so only after her marriage.

9. 'Potpu-Langol' are agricultural tools used in ploughing. Women take part in agriculture in this region. They take part since the transplanting till harvesting. But women are not allowed to touch that 'Potpu-Langol' and again they are not allowed to carry it. They are not allowed to carry 'Papot'- a device to carry articles by using a pole of bamboo where it is placed on the shoulder and the weights are fixed at the two ends of the pole. If a woman touches a 'Potpu-Langol' by mistake or by intention it is believed that the people will face a drought in the coming season.

10. The rims of a 'Yangkok' (winnower) is enforced by strips of cane at several points. When purchasing a 'Yangkok'

the enforcing strips' of cane is counted with the words 'Chak-Nga'. 'And one will purchase it which ends with 'Chak' when counted to the end. In short one has to purchase a 'Yangkok' which ends with an odd number.

11. However, the above norm is just the opposite in purchasing a 'Long' (sieve) for catching fish. One has to purchase a 'Long' which ends with 'Nga' when counting the cane strips with the words 'Chak-Nga'. It means one should buy it which ends with an even number when the whole of the strips are counted.

12. If there are plenty of flowers and fruits in the beginning of the year it is believed that there will be plenty of rain with hailstorm. Further it is believed that the coming season will be stormy. The observation is done in early fruits particularly in mango. In Manipur mango flowers mostly since January and by March fruits are appeared. By observing the amount of flowers and fruits the prediction is made. However, such beliefs has rooms to explain in scientific reasons. In some areas the plants and animals are more sensitive than human beings. It is a way of feeling a stormy weather in advance and preparing for it by producing excessive amount of flowers and fruits.

13. If there is an earthquake in the early morning of Saturday it is believed that the people will face a famine in "future. Further it is believed that a flood is also imminent.

14. If someone fall down when the person is running during an earthquake it is believed that the person will suffer from epilepsy.

15. If a person bites the earth during an earthquake it is believed that the person will possess a strong teeth.

16. If someone shouts with the words 'Chak' 'Chak' during

an earthquake it is believed that the people will enjoy with plenty of foods.

17. 'Nongmangkha' is a medicinal plant. It has a strong bitter taste. People are advised by custom not to go near the plant early in the morning, at noon and at the dusk. If by chance someone faces an evil spirit during the above mentioned time near the 'Nongmangkha' plant it is believed that the person will face death. If someone is forced by circumstance to stand near the plant then the person is further advised by custom to clap for three times while entering near the plant. Further the collection of leaves of the plant on Sunday is prevented by custom. However, the aura of beliefs and practice around this plant has its morale values. Being aware of the extreme medicinal values of the plant it is natural to impose such restrictions so as to protect it from unrestricted collection of the leaves.

18. It is considered unusual to touch the clothing of woman by man. So, much care is taken by both man and woman not to touch their cloths. However, in the time of mating it is a different case. Here, we may examine the reason on two counts; it may be a way of treating woman in subordinate position; the other may be a way of imposing restriction in loose life.

19. A male do not eat the left out food of a woman. It is also unusual to touch a man by woman while he is taking food.

20. It is a practice to clap three times while entering traditional latrine. The belief behind the practice is to ward off evil spirit from the latrine.

21. A men who returns from a journey or from crematorium is welcomed at the gate of the house with a small bonfire. The person has to step upon the fire. It may be due to the

belief that evil spirits may be accompanying the person from his journey or from his way back from crematorium. This practice is very much alive in Manipur.

22. As a custom one will visit when someone is fallen sick or when death occurs to a family. But restriction is imposed to a pregnant woman in visiting the ailing person and on enquiring the death. She is prohibited from doing so as the belief says that bad fortune may occur in the ailing family or in the death occuring family.

REFERENCE

Prepared in consultation with H. Angousana and Ch. Chandramukta of Andro Khunou Leikai.

WITS TEST

Wits Test is popular among the children of Andro. They play on this test when they sit around a hearth in the evening. However, here a process of teaching and learning is involved where the elders are the one who teaches the young ones. This is not a game of mere hide and seek but it certainly involves the exercise of the intellect of the child. In a sense it is a way of sharpening the intellect of the child. Again such tests are oral in nature and so far a written account is not available till date. And it testifies the prevalence of a healthy oral tradition. Such riddles are of various types beginning from very simple to highly literary and complex ones. Following is a selection from the various riddles.

1. Lairabasu Sana Loiba Enak-Khunbasu Sana Loiba karino ?

   Riddle: A poor man also own gold and a rich man also own gold. What is it ?

   Key: Meinee - It is fire. Fire is owned by all the families, both poor and rich.

2. Soraren-gi Machanupa Sori Soraba Mamai Awang Pangna Chaktaba karino ?

   Riddle: Sori Soraba, the son of Soraren, sear,ches its food with his face in the north. What is it ?

Key: Soralune - It is a fish-trap known as 'Soralu'.

3. Loibi Chinggi Chingleibakta houba Shingngen Leirang Magi Ma-U Tabu Yenglaga Pakhang Oibagi Shalloi Shajei Manba Lei, Shingngen Leirang Magi Leina Tabu Yenglaga Kairi Yenkhong Manba Lei, Singngel Leirang Mana Pomlingeidana Likkolgi Tharo Ma-ong Manba Lei, Shingngen Mana Amuk Hanna Shatlagana Lupa Pathap Manba Lei Ashi karino ?

   Riddle: It is a flower which grows on the hill. The stem resembles the whip of a cowboy. Its petal resembles the claw of a cock. When the flower is in bud it looks like a lily. And when it is bloomed it is silvery in colour. What is this flower?

   Key: Lashing - Cotton.

4. Palem Panthougi Shumang Mathoukonda Houba U. Ma-U Tabu Yenglaga Tulsi Bina Devi Manba Lei, Mana Tabu Yenglaga Taoba Huireiton (Huigi Leiton) Manba Lei, Mana Amuk Hanna Shatlagana Pakhang Oibagi Lugun Gaitree Manba Lei, Kari Leino?

   Riddles: It grows in the courtyard of her father. The stem resembles that of Tulsi plant. The leaf looks like the tongue of a dog. But when it blooms it looks like the beads of Lugun (the sacred thread). What is that flower?

   Key: Petruk lei - It is a flower, named 'Petruk Lei'.

5. Loibi Chinggi Chingleipakta Houba Shingel Leirang, Ma-u Tabu Yenglagana Liklai Yumbi Manba Lei, Leina Tabu Yenglagana Kaoren Shan-gi Shankhong Manba Lei, Singngen Mana Pomlingeidana Ningol Magi Khutningthou Manba Lei, Shingngen Leirang Mana Amuk Hanna Shatlagana Nakong Chakra Ma-ong Manba Lei. Loktakishu Hennarei, Napomgishu Ngannarei, Kari Shingngen Leirangno ?

Riddle: It grows in the hill. The stem is like a pillar. The petal looks like the foot of a cow. When it is in bud it look like the ring finger. But when it blooms it resembles the ear hole. It is more pretty than a gorge and it shine on the hill-side. What is this flower?

Key: Chingthrao - A flower in the hill named 'Chingthrao'.

6. Lamlena Patki Patyaida Houba Shingen Leirang, Magi Leina Tabu Yenglagana Panthou Oibagi Khutshu Thanglen Manba Lei, Shingel Mana Pomlingeidana Ningol Oibigi Shinaichei Manba Lei, Shingngel Mana Amuk Hanna Shatlagana Kori Kombandong Lamjen Korika Pakhang Ethak Kanna Lei, Momnu Koloi Paochel Lei, Kari Leirangno ?

   Riddle: It grows in the open field. The leaf of the flower looks like a sword. When it is in bud it resemble the 'Shinaichei' (a stick used in weaving). When it blooms it can excite a youth. It is used in sending message to someone. What is this follower?

   Key: Kombirei - It is a flower named 'Kombirei'.

7. Kangkha Lemphu Karina?

   Riddle: What is that 'Lemphu' under a cot. [Lemphu is the root of water lily etc.]

   Key: Houdong **Mathi** - It is the faeces of a cat.

8. Kalengi Nungsha Phuina Sharagana Leirang Shida Shishina Leirang Nada Nashinna, Ma-U Tabu Yenglagana Panthougi Tongjei Manba Lei, Leina Tabu Yenglagana Chapna Lakoi. Manba Lei,Shingel Mana Pomlingeidana Ningol Oibigi Egani Langdum Maong Manba Lei, Shingel Mana Shatlakandana, Shelotki Tengkot Manba Lei, Ashi Karino ?

Riddle: In the hot summer the flower pretends as dead. The stem looks like the smoking pipe. The leaf looks like a cut out circular banana leaf. When in bud it resembles a thread ball. When in bloom it resembles a bowl. What is that flower?

Key: Thambal - Lotus.

9. Kalen-gi Nungsha Phuina Sharagana Leirang Shida .Shishina Leirang Nada Nashina, Ma-U Tabu Yenglagana Panthougi Tongjei Manba Lei, Leina Tabu Yenglagana Kaoren Sankhong Manba Lei, Shingel Mana Pomlingeidana Ningol Oibigi Egni Langdum Ma-ong Manba Lei, Shingel Mana Shatlakandana Shilotki Tengkot Manba Lei, Ashi Karino ?

Riddles: In the hot sun of summer the flower pretends as dead. The stem looks like the smoking pipe. The leaf resembles the foot of a cow. When in bud it looks like a thread ball. When it is in bloom it resembles a bowl. What is it ?

Key: Tharoni - It is Lily.

10. Leinung Sana Karina?

Riddle: What is underground gold ?

Key: Yaingangni - It is turmeric.

11. Leinung Upu Karino ?

Riddle: What is underground box?

Key: 'Leipakhawaini'- It is groundnut.

12. Mameishu Makokshu Mana Panba Karino ?

Riddle: What is that which has ear on both the head and tail?

Key: Ennaphini -It is the long cloth 'Ennaphi' which has a similar design at both the ends.

REFERENCES

1. Oral interview with Ph.Gopal of Andro Khunou Leikai.
2. Oral interview with Ph. (Ongbi) Salam Ningol Chandrabali of Andro Khunou Leikai.

9

SOCIO-CULTURAL INSTITUTIONS

1. PUJARI AND ARANGPHAM

Pujari and Arangpham are the two social institutions which are closely related to one another. 'Pujaris' are the cooks and 'Arangphams' are the arrangers in a function. Both 'Pujari' and 'Arangpham' are found in Meitei society too but they are not grown as a social institution. Again 'Pujari' and 'Arangpham' are professional in the Meitei society. In Andro there is no professional cooks and arrangers. i.e., no professional 'Pujari' and 'Arangpham'. So 'Pujari' and 'Arangpham' are needed to be recruited from their society only. From such a situation the two institutions 'Pujari' and 'Arangpham' has flourished.

A. Pujaris

Community feast is a regular feature in Andro community. For such feasts cooks are needed and the same is provided by the institution 'Pujari'. So 'Pujaris' (cooks) are recruited from their youths. And a youth who has attained 17/18 years of age is recruited to 'Pujari'. As a tradition in Andro a male youth who has attained seventeen or eighteen years of age is compulsorily admitted to either of the two institutions. He will continue to be in this institution till he attain 40 years of age.

The retirement of senior 'Pujaris' and admission of young 'pujaris are confirmed by a function known as 'Pujari Channaba'- which is held after every three years on the sixteenth day of 'Kalen' (April-May) month. The day is invariably the next day of 'Kalen-gi Purnima' i.e. the full moon day of May. For the year 2003 it was held on 17.05.03. These 'Pujaris' and 'Arangphams' are not independent organisations, rather they are part and parcel of the village administration. It is under the strict supervision of 'Loishang', the fountainhead of the village administration. Consequent to this style of recruitment of youths to both the institutions there are hundreds of 'Pujaris' and 'Arangbas' in the village. Based on the record maintained by the 'Pujari Loishang' (dept.) there are 637 'Pujaris' on 17.05.03. after deducting the retiring 40 senior 'Pujaris'.

Involvement of Pujaris in Social and Familial Functions

In Andro death ceremony is performed with a feast. Again another feast is held on the death anniversary of the person. The 'Pujaris' from 'Pujari Shang' (dept.) will cook in such feasts. Feast is also included in 'Langban Chak-Khangba'- a ritual observance held every year in the month of 'Langban' (Sept.) in remembrance of a deceased. In this occasion also 'Pujaris' will help the family in cooking. Further they also help on catering food. But informing the 'Pujaris' needs a certain procedure and one cannot do so by bypassing the same. Both the 'Arangba' and 'Pujari' are available in a given Leikai (local). The concern family first of all inform the 'Arangbas' in the local. The 'Arangba' in turn will visit the concern family. The family will ask the required number of 'Pujaris' for the particular occasion. The 'Arangbas' in turn will invite the 'Pujaris' with flowers. Traditionally flower was used in invitation not only in Andro but among the Meiteis also. The 'Pujaris' after taking their meal visits the concerned family in the night. They will spend the night at the verandah of the house. This they do in order to facilitate in starting their work early in the morning. Over and above this the 'Pujaris' perform their duties at the village or community level functions.

Pujari Channaba

It is a function which is held every after three years. It is held on the 16th day of 'Kalen' (May). On this day a forty (40) senior 'Pujaris' retire and another forty (40) are promoted to occupy their vacant place from the junior 'Pujaris'.

Again on this day young 'Pujaris' are also recruited who has attained the required age. The strength of the senior 'Pujaris' are kept maintain at eighty (80). This they do by promoting another forty (40) from the junior 'Pujaris' when forty (40) senior 'Pujaris' retire on the occasion of 'Pujari Channaba'.

For a successful performance of the function which is held every after three years a well organised preparation was made many days ahead of the day of the occasion. Rice bear is the main attraction of food item in the function. So rice bear is prepared in large quantity by engaging more than twenty 'Yu Kharung' (jars) a few days before the function. Then comes the collection of 'La' (banana leaves) and 'Khangla Mana', the leaves of 'Khangla' tree. This 'Khangla' leaves are collected from the hills. 'Khangla' leaf is involved in many rites and rituals of the Andros. 'Shingju' (vegetable palao) is another essential food item of the function. So they boil a large amount of 'Mangal' (peas) for preparing 'Shingju'. But what is interesting is the social division of labour in its traditional form. The young 'Pujaris' are divided into various groups and every group is assigned a particular task.

For example a group assigned to collect 'La' (banana leaf) is named as 'Laroi'. So the collection of 'La', 'Khangla Mana' (Khangla leaves) and fetching of water from the pond are done by different groups of young 'Pujaris'. Again at the time of catering food, the same is executed by other remaining groups. So catering of 'Yu' (rice bear) and 'Shingju' are assigned to different groups of remaining young 'Pujaris'.

The function opens with a ritual offering of 'Yu' (bear) to deity in the early morning by womenfolk of the locality whic:h is known as 'Yu Thaba'. However, the function begins at around, 3.30 p.m. in the afternoon. Many elders of the village are present in the occasion. The presence of the 'Khullakpa', among others, the members of the Loishang, is a necessity. Their presence is vital because they are the one who will extend permission to retire the forty (40) senior 'Pujaris' and promote another, (40) to senior 'Pujaris' from the junior 'Pujaris'. The stage of the function is on the verandah of the house while the members of the 'Loishang' and the crowd sits in the courtyard and in the out houses (Shangoi). The young boys who are to be admitted *to* the institution on the occasion are allowed to sit together in a selected place. The function opens with an opening song sung by a ballad singer who sings the ballad 'Khamba - Thoibi' of Moirang, a principality of the then kingship located at the south western side of the Imphal Valley. The performance is on the verandah of the house where a simple offering is displayed including an earthen jar. He sings with the accompaniment of a traditional drum known as 'Dholok'. What is interesting is the inclusion of 'Phibul'-the traditional whip prepared by a white cloth.

The same is placed exposed on a banana leaf near the offering. It is a symbol of authority, discipline and orderliness. And anyone who misbehaves during the ceremony will be tamed with blows from the 'Phibul'

A group of senior 'Pujaris' seeking permission for retirement in 'Pujari Channaba.'

A Junior 'Pujari' seeking admission in 'Pujari Loishang' on the day of 'Pujari Channaba.'

What follows after the ballad is the process of admission of the youths to the institution. The new recruits are allowed to wear the 'Khudei' (loin cloth) only but the top remain bare. Each one has to present a song of his desire to the crowd. Of course, for this purpose there is a mike and a few musical instruments. Each one will come up on the stage and will present the song. In the course they are assisted by two seniors who wear 'Khaon' shirt (traditional shirt made by a white Khudei-Ioin cloth) with their traditional head gears. Before presenting the song, anyone picked up from the various local songs, he will prostate to the elders and the crowd. While singing he will wear a garland made of green leaves of 'Tairen' tree. The garland is prepared not by thread but by 'Paya'- bamboo chips. While singing he is assisted by some simple instruments. The custom is continued not without its merits, it has its merit in making the boy sociable. In fact such a function is a training ground of instilling discipline among the youths. Certainly it is a place where the youths are trained on how to behave to their elders and vice-versa by the elders to the youths. When he finishes the song he will exclaims with words 'Eyambashing Loiyjare' - meaning that he has finished singing the song. Before leaving the stage he will do another prostate to the elders of the village as well as to the crowd. While leaving the stage he will leave the garland of 'Tairen' leaves. The same is garlanded to the next persons who will also present a song to the crowd. Thus the admission of a youth to either of the two institutions i.e. 'Pujari' and 'Arangpham' may be interpreted as performing their puberty rite. The only difference is that it has become functional. Performing one's function in the society is indicative of the stage of one's life. Now it has indicated that the boy's have attained their puberty. While the function is in progress a group of 'Pujaris' will perform the duty of 'Dolai Paba'. They do their duty of policing. In fact the 'Dolai Paba' is the traditional police in the erstwhile kingship. Each one is armed with a long bamboo stick; a symbol of orderliness. They are empowered to control anyone who misbehaves during the function. They will walk around the venue of the function. If anyone is found behaving against the custom of keeping order during the function the matter is immediately referred to the 'Pujari Ahan' - the seniormost 'Pujari'. If the 'Pujari Ahan' is unable to bring the person under his control then he refers the matter to 'Loishang'- the village authority. He is forced to prostate on the ground and will be thrashed by 'Phibul' - the traditional whip. The blows are not severe one to make mark on the back but to make feel ashame of his action.

Having finished the part played by the young recruit on the stage now the turn has come for the retiring senior 'Pujaris'. The retiring senior 'Pujaris' will come up on the verandah, the stage, and remain kneeling on the ground with their folding hands asking the permission from 'Khullakpa' - chief of the village. They remain kneeling facing the east while the crowd is facing west. With a word of accepting their request to retire from the 'Khullakpa' the senior 'Pujaris' change their kneeling position to lying prostate on the ground with their folded hands. At this stage 'Epa Khullakpa' leaves his seat and comes up on the stage and slide down each one of the senior 'Pujaris' on their heads. The action of 'Khullakpa' is symbolic of accepting their request, to retire. With the due permission to retire from the 'Epa Khullakpa' the retiring 'Pujaris' moves down from the stage to the courtyard and shows their reverence to the elders by bowing to each one of them. 'Epa Khullakpa' in turn delivers his concluding remarks who gives due emphasis on the custom and tradition of the 'Chakpas'in general and the Andros in particular. He gives his words to sustain their age-old tradition and culture despite the manyfold activities of modern age. Thus the gathering comes to an end with the serving of 'Shingju' and rice bear to all those present on the occasion - serving the 'Shingju' on 'Khangla Mana' - the 'Khangla' leaves.

B. ARANGPHAM

As mentioned earlier 'Arangpham' is another social institution of the youths who works in tandem with the 'Pujaris' in the familial and social functions in the village.

But their function is somewhat lighter than the 'Pujaris'. They are the arrangers or managers in a function of a family or of the village or community. Their duty ranges from relaying message for a function in a family, preparing of Athenpots of fruits and flowers for different types of functions and offering 'Lei Chandan' to the visitors in a function etc.

Like the 'Pujaris' they are also recruited at the early age of seventeen or eighteen years and remain in the organisation till he attain the age of forty (40). Again there are senior eighty (80) 'Arangbas' where a half of it (40) retires on a function known as 'Arangpham Channaba' which is held every after three years on the third day of 'Kalen' (April-May). On this day a number of young recruits are also admitted into the organisation. With the retirement of forty (40) senior 'Arangbas' on this occasion another forty (40) junior 'Arangbas' are promoted to fill up the space left by the retirement of the forty (40) senior 'Arangbas'. So the number of senior 'Arangbas' is kept unchanged at eighty (80).

A feature worthwhile is that the designated day for the observance of 'Arangpham Channaba' and 'Pujari Channaba' is reversible and is not held on the same day as was held in the previous year. As for instance the 'Arangpham Channaba' which was held on third day of 'Kalen' (April-May), 2003 cannot be held on this same day on the next observance which fall on May, 2006. It is shifted to sixteenth day of Kalen (April-May), 2006. On the other side 'Pujari Channaba' which was observed on the sixteenth day of 'Kalen' (April-May), 2003 is shifted to third day of 'Kalen' (April-May), 2006. The cycle continues in this way till date.

The procedure of observing 'Arangpham Channaba' is almost the same with that of 'Pujari Channaba' which includes the opening with 'Yu Thaba' - ritual offering of 'Yu' (liquor) in the early morning, beginning of function in the afternoon with an opening song by a ballad singer, offering of songs by new recruits, blessing by 'Khullakpa' to the retiring senior 'Arangbas', policing the function by 'Dolai Pabas', etc.

However, in the concluding part a difference crops up with the inclusion of 'Ningols' (unmarried girls) of the village in the function. Each girl contribute a minimum amount of Rs. 10/- to the function. Most of the time they remain as audience but they take part in preparing 'Shingju' (raw vegetable palao) for the occasion. With the inclusion of girls of the village in the occasion the function 'Arangpham Channaba' attracts a huge crowd.

SHINNAIPHAM KABA

Andro society is a male dominated society where women are excluded from most of the rituals and ceremonies. But it does not mean that women remain secluded in their houses. Their share in the economic life of the Andro society is commendable and there are areas which are reserved for them. As for instance pottery, textile industry, preparing beverage and fishing, etc. are their areas of economic activity. They also share their labour in rice cultivation. As mentioned earlier boys are trained to cultivate discipline and make them sociable in the institutions like 'Arangpham' and 'Pujari', etc; Likewise Andro society do not neglect their girls and for them also there is the institution named 'Shinnaipham Kaba'. In literal meaning 'Shinnaipham' is workshed and 'Kaba' is to attend the workshed. But it is more than a workshed and it also serves a place to cultivate discipline and to make them sociable. Again the girls do not assemble in a separate house as suggested by the term "Shinnaipham" but girls numbering around four or five will gather in a spacious house in their neighbourhood. The favourite room in the house is the 'Ningol ka' - the room for the girls. So there are numbers of 'Shinnaiphams' in a locality and many more in the Andro

Village. The elderly woman of the house in which they assemble is their teacher. She is the one who will teach them the long process of weaving beginning from extracting raw material to producing a cloth. However, a divorcee is not allowed to attend such a place. The girls will attend the workshed along with their required raw materials, tools and implements like spinning wheel, loin-loom, ginning machine (Kaptreng), etc. For cotton the process of weaving begins from ginning followed by carding, cotton rolling (Moithap Taba), Spinning (Lang Naiba) and Winding. Finally the thread from 'Langkhai' - hank is twisted around a wooden or bamboo bobbin by a process known as 'Langchak-Chakpa' which is done by a machine known as Tareng (Spinning Wheel). The use of different tools and implements involved in the process beginning from ginning to producing a thread filled bobbin which needs different skills at each stage is taught in the workshed. It does not end here and they are also taught to weave in a loin-loom as well as in a handloom. But for the experienced one they will work here to produce a thread filled bobbin or a cloth. The activity do not end here, some of the girls use to engage in rice pounding. Again the visit by the boys in the workshed in the night after taking their meals transforms the environment of the workshed from a place of economic activity to a social institution. The boys will mix with the girls and they will chat, sing and play in wits test, etc.

The boys will also help the girls in rice pounding. In return the girls use to treat the boys with traditional pipe-smoking (Nganthak Thakpa, Hidak Thakpa). However, the boys will leave the place at around 10/11 p.m. .and they are not allowed to spend the night in the house. But the girls use to spend the night in the workshed and return to their respective houses in the morning. In the midst of this whole activity in the workshed the elderly women of the house educate the young girls on their behaviour and discipline to be maintained in their houses as well as those to be maintained in their married life. They are also taught to lead hygienic life in the time of their monthly cycles, the relationship to be maintained with their husbands in such a period, etc.

REFERENCES

1. Prepared after participating the function on 17-05-03 with the added information from the 'Pujari Ahan', Ph. Chandra and N.Shyam, both from Andro, Mamang Leikai.

2. Oral interview with Ch. Palandro of Andro Khunou Leikai.

10

CALENDAR OF RITUALS AND FESTIVALS

A number of community based rituals and festivals are held in Andro in most of the months in a year. Excepting the four months, viz. 'Wakching' (January), Enga (June), Engel (July) and Poinu (December) all the remaining eight months are engaged in one or more rituals in a year. However, there are categories of rituals and festivals considering their cycle of performance. There is a group of rituals which are held regularly every year in its usual calendar, e.g. 'Khunthong Latpa', 'Laisha Tanba', Cheiraoba, Langban Chak-Khangba, Lam Haiba, Kurak Lamtaiba, Leichreng Leitaba, Leipak Leithong Hangba, and Loutaba, etc. There are festivals which are held every after three years; they are 'Pujari Channaba' and 'Arangpham Channaba', etc. Again there are festivals which are held only when there is the need to perform the festival. The major festivals, 'Panam Haraoba' and 'Pureiromba Haraoba', are held only when their arises the need to perform the festival. As a necessary condition the festival is performed only when their shrine is broken due to old age. The ritual 'Maibi Chaklon Katpa' is such a ritual which will remain performing as long as the festivals 'Panam' and 'Pureiromba Haraoba' is not held in the village. .This ritual is a substitute of the two 'Haraoba' festivals. There will be no such ritual in the year when there is 'Panam' and

'Pureiromba Haraoba' festivals. But the ritual immediately resumes in the next year when there is no 'Haraoba' festival which is difficult to decide its next timing. Again, here, a change environment is that the shrine is replaced by modern concrete building which will last many years. Formerly the shrine was made by bamboo and thatch roofs which parishes after five or six years. The shrine for 'Pureiromba' and 'Chingshomba' are also being replaced by modern concrete buildings. So it is difficult to decide under which circumstance the festivals can be held. Questions can arise why there is no rituals and festivals in December, January and June, July? The reason is not far to seek for June and July, because these are the two months when the villagers are heavily engaged in cultivation. It is such a time when the villagers are unable to spare even a moment for other engagement. So naturally there cannot be ritual and festival in these months. On the other side, December and January are relatively free months, free from the hectic activity of rice cultivation. Again these are the two months when there are plenty of harvest, harvested from the labour of June and July. But why not a ritual or a festival in such relatively wealthy and free months? Does the rituals and festivals are conditioned and determined by agricultural cycle?

The calendar of ritual open on 'Fairen-gi Mangani Panba' - the fifth day of 'Fairen' (January-February). On this day two rituals are held early in the morning; one is 'Loutaba' and the other is 'Leipak Leithong Hangba'. Khunthong Latpa' and 'Laisha Tanba' are held in 'Lamta' (February-March). It is on the first 'Thangja' (Saturday) of 'Lamta' that 'Khunthong Latpa' is performed in the evening in the dark. Immediately on the next day, i.e, on the first 'Nongmaiching' (Sunday) the ritual hunting 'Laisha Tanba' is executed. 'Panam Haraoba' festival is also held in this month 'Lamta' (February-March). The month 'Shachiphu' (March-April) witness the celebration of 'Cheiraoba'- the new year which is held on 'Shachiphu -Nongma Panba'-the first day of 'Shachiphu' (March-April). Again a hordes of celebrations are held in the month of 'Kalen' (April-May), On the third day of 'Kalen' (April-May) the Andros will go for a pilgrimage on 'Nongmaiching' hill for a prayer to 'Pakhangba Surung'. Again on this day either of the festivals 'Pujari Channaba' or 'Arangpham Chanaba' is held. It is on the sixteenth day of 'Kalen' that one of the above two festivals is held according to their traditional roster. The month 'Thawan' (July-August) witness the celebration of the ritual 'Maibi Chaklon Katpa'. And this is followed by 'Langban Chak-Khangba' and 'Lam Haiba' in "Langban' (August-September). The two rituals 'Leichreng Leitaba' and 'Kurak Lamtaiba' is performed in 'Mera' (September-October) month. The festival 'Ningol Chak-Kouba' is held in Hiyang-gei (October-November). The following is a discussion of the rituals and festivals of Andro community in a calendar year.

A. FAIREN (JANUARY-FEBRUARY)

Loutaba and Leipak Leithong Hangba

1. Loutaba

This ritual is performed in early morning in one's paddy field. It is a simple prayer which includes the offering of a chicken. The offering is done at one corner of the field. As mentioned earlier the ritual is held on the fifth day of 'Fairen' (January-February) month. The prayer is simple and pray for a good harvest for the comming year. As a tradition a farmer is allowed to work in the field after the ritual. Before this ritual, as a custom farmers do not work in the field in Andro. Such a tradition existed in other areas of Manipur at one time, but it is no longer available in other areas beyond the Andro village. Even the term 'Loutaba' is disappearing from the Meitei society. Thanks to the sense of preservation of custom and tradition of the Andro community.

2. Leipak Leithong Hangba

Leipak Leithong Hangba is a ritual which is held side by side with 'Loutaba' on the same day and around the same time early in the morning. It is a ritual, which inaugurates the collection of 'Leitan' (clay) from the traditional site of 'Leitan' (clay) known as 'Leitanpekpham'. The ritual is discussed at length at another chapter relating to pottery.

B. LAMTA (FEBRUARY-MARCH)

1. Khunthong Latpa

In Manipur the Meiteis perform a ritual named 'Sharoi Khangba' on the first 'Thangja' (Saturday) of 'Lamta' (March). The same ritual is performed on the second 'Thangja' of 'Lamta' and thus completes the ritual. 'Saroi Khangba' in fact, is a ritual of offering foods to evil spirits known as 'Sharoi' so as not to bring harm to the population around the area in the ensuing year. The food includes rice, salt, chilli, vegetables of the season, etc. So it is a ritual propitiating the evil spirits. But the Andros perform the ritual as "Khunthong Latpa'. At one point of time the Meiteis also termed this ritual as 'Khunthong Latpa'.

'Khunthong Latpa' ritual may be divided into two parts, one in the morning and the other at the dusk, in the evening. In the morning part two chickens are sacrificed, one at the alter of 'Panam Ningthou' and the other at the shrine of 'Pureiromba'. The sacrifice is executed by the 'Laipus' (the persons in charge of the deities) of the respective deities. But while sacrificing the chickens a colour code is maintained, and hence a reddish chicken for the 'Panam' and a white one for the 'Pureiromba'. The associated item in the sacrifice which is traditionally known as 'Yelhing Thaba' is the 'Yu' (liquor).

Again the 'Yu' is of two kinds; one is 'Puk- Yu' and the other is 'Lai- Yu', 'Pukyu' is the rice bear, 'Laiyu' is not fit for consumption and is made by putting a piece of 'Hamei' (yeast) in plane water. The sacrifice include a hog also. While killing the hog it is done by a device known as 'Upan Chanba' but not by hitting hard on the head. It is a simple device designed to crush the hog to death by two wooden posts. One end of the two wooden posts is tied tightly and the other side is left free. The hog is put inside near the tied end and it is crushed by three, four persons to death from the other end. The hog is slit open and the 'Pei' (liver) is carefully removed. The shape, size and nature of the 'Pei' is observed carefully and tries to forecast something pertaining to rain., disease, drought, war and peace, etc. in the coming seasons of the year. This is termed as 'Shapei Yengba'. Both the hog and rice is cooked as early as possible. The necessary chickens involved in the ritual 'Yelhing Thaba' are contributed by 'Loishang' - the village authority. However, the search of the chickens are assigned to the Nambors- who does a kind of orderly work in the village administration. The seven office beares of 'Loishang' are also involved in the ritual 'Yelhing Thaba'. Besides elderly persons of the village also take part in the ritual. The ingredients in the ritual are seven different kinds of fruits, seven different kinds of flowers, "Shingju of Heibimana" (vegetable palao of Heibi leaves), rice and 'Thoiding', etc.

Subsequent to the performance of 'Yelhing Thaba' ritual in the morning then the ritual 'Khunthong Latpa' is held in the evening in the dusk. However, the collection of necessary items for the ritual began a day before the day of ritual. The collection of the necessary items from each and every house is an act of facilitating the 'Maibas' (priests) to carry away the dirt and filth from the house so as to place before the deity for his disposal. Here the 'Maibas' are the pleader, pleading to the deity for a favour of the villagers. The collection of rice is assigned to 'Pana' members of the respective 'Leikai' (local). The 'Nambors' are not engaged in this matter. A task force comprising five to ten persons are assigned for the collection. And such a group is known as 'Shintha'.

As a *tradition a person is compulsorily admitted to 'Pana' administration when he completes six months after his marriage. His initial admission to 'Pana' is termed* as *'Thou Kaba'. However, he becomes* a *full fledged member of 'Pana' division only when the ritual 'Hirukaba' is performed in the 'Pana' house known as 'Panashang'. On this day the office bearers of 'Loishang', the 'Nambors', 'Pana Pannaba' (the person is charge of the Panshang) and the elders of the concerned family are present in the occasion. However, women do not figure in the scene.*

This ritual 'Khunthong Latpa' is performed at a time when most of the villagers have returned to their houses. And the same is held at four points of the village, i.e. at the east, west, north and south extremities of the village. For this, as a custom, four 'Maibas' (priests) are involved in the ritual for the four points. A number of elderly persons also follow the 'Maibas'.

The villagers are scared of such a ritual and always try to avoid encountering such a scene. Again it is the authority who forbids anyone on coming across the ritual. However, anyone who accidentally encounters a procession of 'Maibas' and elderly persons who are marching with chicken and other items of the ritual is pardoned and is let free without any punishment. But for those who encounters the ritual when it is in progress then definitely a fine is imposed. One has to pay the fine in cash. Though the amount is small what is implied is that the 'Maiba' is pleading for a good health and a long life of the person. It is such a ritual in which the villagers as well as outsiders are forbidden to witness the scene. Again chances of observing it secretly is also bleak as it is held in the dark. So a list of involved items cannot be prepared besides the chicken. However, it is certain that a small amount of 'Yu' (liquor) is included. After offering the chicken to deity then it is sacrificed by cutting its neck. The chicken is finally buried in the ground. *In Andro women are not involved in the ritual. But the opposite is the case among the Meiteis. In 'Sharoi Khangba' of the Meiteis it is the women who perform the ritual.* The four 'Maibas' along with the elderly persons who accompanied them in the ritual returns to 'Loishang' after executing their duties at the four extremities of the village, i.e. at north, south, east and west. They along with the office bearers of the 'Loishang' enjoy the feast of pork. And thus concludes the ritual.

The first 'Thangja' (Saturday) of 'Lamta' (March) is treated as the separating point of two seasons; ending of winter .and beginning of spring. In such a point of time it is prayed to God to carry away all the dirt and filth from the village to southerly direction. Further prayed to God for a prosperous and healthy year for the village.

2. Laisha Tanba (Hunting for the Deity)

This is an occasion of community hunting where the hunted is offered to their principal deity, the 'Panam Ningthou'. Every year the ritual 'Khunthong Latpa' is held on the first 'Thangja' (Saturday) of 'Lamta' (March) month. On the next day i.e. on the first 'Nongmaiching' (Sunday) of 'Lamta' (March) the community celebrates the 'Laisha Tanba' a hunting mission. The favourite animal for the occasion is a stag. So the hunting is carried out for two to three days till the favourite game in hunted. However, the chance capture of another animal is also accepted. .

In the case of a failure to capture any game then a hog is sacrificed in lieu of the failure. The participants in the game are the married persons who are members of the 'Pana' division. As a custom the 'Khangjengs' (bachelors) are excluded in the hunting. But this is relaxed for the few who are interested in hunting. Even old persons are allowed to take part in the hunting. And a 'Pana' member can take part in the hunting as long as his health permits. And one can retire oneself from such participation if his health desires to do so. There is no fault in the tradition as this would be continued by the able bodied persons. However, in the past the custom was strictly enforced and anyone who failed to participate in the hunting was punished in the form of a fine. The authority used to send the 'Nambors' to collect the fine from the absentees.

A gathering before the hunting expedition in the ritual hunting 'LAISHA TANBA.'

The hunting is executed under certain planning and organisation. At the initial stage it is 'the Nambors' who appoint the 'Sharois' who are constituted by seven to eight persons. The 'Sharois' are the advance party and their task is to locate an animal in the forest. These 'Sharois' are sent early in the morning to locate the animal in deep forest where one may easily find out an animal. They will search the animal in the traditional hunting grounds like 'Khanglahoubi', 'Shaphonglok', etc. The advance party went without food. Their share is brought as 'Chakyom' (packed food) by his close friends or relatives. The advance party return from the forest after locating an animal. They will return upto 'Lamphelshoi'- the extremity of the village in the east, and wait for their food. They will take food there (at Lamphelshoi) from the 'Chakyom' brought by the rear party. After their food both the advance and rear party proceed for the forest in the hill.

A brief preparation is made before advancing for hunting in the hill. A small offering is made to the deity who is considered in charge of the area. And the simple offering include banana (a hand), egg, 'Yu' (liquor), water, Kabok (puffed rice) and betel nuts and leaves. The whole items are put on a broad 'Khangla Mana' (leaf of Khangla tree). The simple prayer is for an easy capture of an animal without any accident.

After the simple prayer the participants are gathered in the field and those assembled are roughly divided into two groups namely 'Shathouba Kangbu' and 'Sharumba Kangbu'. This is a strategy to hunt and finally to catch the animal. The 'Shathouba' are the hunters and they will encircle the area and hunt the animal to a particular direction. The 'Sharumba' are the one who remain hiding in the probable escape routes of the animal. They will ambush the animal while escaping from the hunting. The traditional hunting weapons are sword, spear, bow and arrow. However, this is modernised with the inclusion of barrel gun (single). An elderly person of those assembled makes a war cry and gives his directives on how to proceed in the hunting. In compliance to his directives the 'Shathouba' and 'Sharumba' rushes to their respective directions. The hunted animal from such a venture is brought home on a device known as 'Potpu'. Now the game is kept hanging on another device known as 'Shayan U' at the premises of 'Loishang'- the fountainhead of village administration. The message is relayed throughout the village by beating the traditional drum in its usual tune. Such a drum and tune is known as "Shapao Pung". In no time the villagers gather at the 'Loishang' ground to witness the captured game. If sufficient time is available the game is cooked on the same day. If not the same is cooked on the next day. The cooked pieces are distributed to those present in the ground. These small pieces are known as 'Laigi Sharou'. Children are the favourites of the cooked pieces. Rice is not included in the distribution. Only the cooked pieces are distributed to those present in the ground and not at the homes.

In exceptional cases the villagers fail to capture an animal. In such a situation an animal is sacrificed in lieu of the failure. And the animal is a hog. A hog is purchased and the same is kept hanging on the 'Shayan U'. After the sacrificial ritual the hog is killed and the same is cooked. The message is relayed by means of 'Paothang' not by beating drums. The cooked pieces are distributed in the like manner to all those gathered at the 'Loishang'. Thus the simple ceremony terminates at the ground of 'Loishang'.

3. Panam Haraoba

It is also held in this month 'Lamta', but it is discussed in a separate chapter.

C. SHACHIPHU (MARCH-APRIL)[3]

Cheiraoba

The new year day is celebrated on the 'Shachiphu Nongma Panba'- the first day of 'Shachiphu' (March-April) month. The celebration is held in the morning and it is short and simple. Offering is made at three places; one in the courtyard another at the south-western side of the house and lastly at the gate of the house.

Offering at the gate of house on 'Cheiraoba'-The New Year

At the Courtyard

An offering space is made at the north-eastern corner of the courtyard which is termed as 'Shumang'. While offering the cooked food one has to face north. The offering include the cooked vegetable of the season, meat (pork), fish and chicken etc. 'Yu' (liquor) is compulsorily included. What is offered in this space is not to deity but a share for the souls of the deceased members of the family. It is prayed to the souls to enjoy the foods offered on this new year day.

At Shanthong

The above items of food are offered at this place also i.e. at 'Shanthong'- the south-western side of the house. Here one is asking for a long life from the deity- 'Wangbren Khana Chaoba'. If any member of the family is included in the list of death persons; it is asked from the deity to exclude he or she from the list. In other words it is prayed to the deity of death not to bring death in the family in the coming year.

At Konthong

Last of all the offering is made at the gate of the house.

While offering the above items of food one faces the south. The offering is made to the deity 'Lamhaba Tuhaba Lam Shemba Tu Shemba Lamshi Lamkoiba'. It is prayed to enjoy the offered food and in return to carry away all the dirt and filth and diseases from the house to the southerly direction. A healthy, wealthy and long life is begged from the deity.

As a next step the 'Eshaiphu' (pitcher) of 'Leimaren' (household female deity) is cleaned with water after taking food. This is cleaned by a woman of the family who is free from monthly cycle. If she is during the monthly cycle she cannot do the job. Again the cleaning is done inside the house. After cleaning it is filled with sacred water. It is garlanded with the leaves of 'Tairen' tree. A small offering of fruits and betel nuts and leaves is made to it.

D. KALEN (APRIL-MAY)[4]

1. Pakhangba Surung Kaba

On the tbird day of 'Kalen' (April-May) the Andros will go for a pilgrimage on the 'Nongmaiching' hill for a prayer to 'Pakhangba Surung'. This occasion is known as 'Pakhangba Surung Kaba'. Here 'Surung' means cave and this cave is believed to be housed by 'Pakhangba' deity. This pilgrimage is not so popular even among the Andros. One reason is the difficulty in scaling the height at the high of summer.

2. Pujari Channaba and Arangpham Channab

These ritual festival's are also held in the month 'Kalen' (April–May), however, both of them are discussed in a separate chapter.

E. THAWAN (JULY-AUGUST)

1. Maibi Chaklong Katpa

As a tradition the Andros perform the ritual festivals

'Panam Haraoba' and 'Pureiromba Haraoba' in 'February-March' and 'April-May'. However, these ritual festivals of their principal deities could not be held every year because of one reason or the other. One basic reason is that such festivals are performed only when their shrine is broken due to old age. In such a situation in lieu of the above two ritual festivals the ritual 'Maibi' 'Chaklon Katpa' is held on the first 'Nongmaiching' (Sunday) of 'Thawan' (July-August) month. The main part of the ritual is held at the shrine of 'Pureiromba' deity early in the morning which include a ceremony known as 'Maibi Hiru Kaba'. The latter part of the ritual is held at the residence of 'Pureiromba Laipu' - the 'Maiba' (priest) in charge of the deity. However, the day long ceremony is accomplished only when the 'Loishang' grants its ritual assurance to do so.

The Andros has a tradition of maintaining the institution of 'Maibi'the priestess. Traditionally they have thirteen 'Maibis' selected from thirteen lineages. These thirteen Maibis are in charge of thirteen different 'Umanglais' (sylvan deities). However, these thirteen 'Umanglais' are a selection from the 363 'Umanglais' of Manipur. These thirteen 'Maibis' are under a definite order where the 'Maibi' in charge of 'Pureiromba' is treated as the seniormost. The juniormost being the 'Maibi' in charge of 'Penakhongbi' deity. This order cannot be disturbed in any circumstance. Since the ancient past the women of these lineages hold the charge of 'Maibi'. Their place cannot be replaced by a woman from another lineage. In a lineage of many 'Mous' (women) the eldest will hold the charge of 'Maibi' as long as she desires. In the event of her retirement or expiry the next elder will hold the post.

The lineages of the 'Maibis' who are in charge of the thirteen different 'Umanglais' can be arranged in the following manner.

LIST OF UMANGLAIS	—	LIST OF THE LINEAGES
1. Pureiromba	—	Sharungbam Ongbi
2. Chingshomba	—	Sharubam Ongbi
3. Panam	—	Asheibam Ongbi
4. Sanahongba	—	Phanjoubam Ongbi
5. Korouhanba	—	Thokchom Ongbi
6. Chaningleima	—	Yumkhaibam Ongbi
7. Thonglenlakpa	—	Chingakham Ongbi
8. Sanglenlakpa	—	Chingakham Ongbil
9. Peng Gurutlai	—	Shagolshem Ongbi/Ningol
10. Soraren	—	Heikrujam Ongbi
11. Meirathanbi	—	Ningthoujam Ongbi
12. Uranlakpa	—	Puthem Ongbi
13. Penakhongbi	—	Salam Ongbi

The ritual 'Maibi Chaklon Katpa', though it is held on the first 'Nongmaiching' (Sunday) of 'Thawan' (July-August) at early morning, however, a preparation was made a few days ahead of the occasion.

Like in the rituals where there is an active involvement of 'Loishang' in one form or the other, the initiative to perform the ritual also comes from the 'Loishang'. The 'Nambor' of the village, who acts more than a watchman and messenger, will inform to the 'Maiba Ahan' (the head priest) a few days ahead of the last Sunday of 'Engen' (June-July) on the ensuing ritual. 'Maiba Ahan' relays the message to 'Maibi Ahan'. Further the 'Maibi Ahan' will inform to the remaining

'Maibis'. Subsequently a meeting is held on the last Sunday of 'Engen' (June–July) at the house of 'Maibi Ahan' with an agenda to hold the ritual. In execution of the decision emerged out of the meeting the 'Maibis' make a search to purchase a hog. The cost of the hog is contributed by the 'Maibis' themselves. However, the hog is very selective as it should not be a defective one. An animal with a broken leg or ear or tail is not considered for the offering in the ritual. Maibis will inform the 'Maiba Ahan' on the availability of the hog. In case a suitable hog is not found out then the 'Maibis' in the right earnest make the 'Loishang' aware of the situation. In order not to happen any break in the tradition the ritual is delayed by a week, only to be held on the second Sunday of 'Thawan' (July-August). Till now there is not such incident of not finding a suitable hog for the purpose. It is certain to get such a hog as the village is big enough to get the same. However, this is an option not to meet any break in the tradition.

A scene of 'Maibi Hiru Kaba.'

Fig. Maibis in action as a preparation for the ritual 'Maibi Chaklon Katpa.'

Preparation for the ritual is made some days ahead of the first Sunday by contributing three 'Meruks' (a measuring pot for rice) of rice by each and every 'Maibi' only to be deposited to the house of 'Maibi Ahan'. If any 'Maibi' deposits exceeding the three 'Meruks' of rice, then the excess is returned to the same person. Depending upon the prevailing situation the rice so 'contributed by the 'Maibis' is again redistributed to the thirteen 'Maibis' in the same amount of three 'Meruks' that they contributed. The 'Maibis' in turn will convert the rice into flour at their respective homes. Or the contributed rice is kept at the house of 'Maibi Ahan' for safe custody till Sunday when they together will convert it to flour in the early hour of Sunday. In the event of redistribution of the contributed rice the flour so converted from it is deposited again at the house of 'Maibi Ahan' at the early hour of Sunday, preferably before 4 a.m. While depositing rice they also accompany a certain amount of firewood for use in cooking the whole items, e.g. the flour and meat, etc. In the next step while depositing the flour they also bring a small amount of salt and chilli. However, it excludes mustard oil. With the gathering of the necessary persons along with the items they contribute then the 'Maiba Ahan' or 'Pureiromba Laipu' leads a procession to the precinct of 'Pureiromba' shrine. They also carry the sacrificial hog in the procession. At about the same time the 'Maibi' (a junior one) for whom the ritual 'Hiru Kaba' is to be performed is arrived at the shrine. This ritual 'Hiru Kaba' promotes a novice 'Maibi' to a full fledged 'Maibi'. So naturally such a 'Maibi' is a junior 'Maibi'. After this ritual she can offer ritual service to a deity. For the ritual the necessary items like rice bear, and a cock besides other ingredients, e.g. 'Khongdrum Khongkha' (an unedible gourd) and Heimang Maton (buds of Heimang tree), ginger, and a roasted Ngamu (a fish) for 'Shingpak Shingju' etc. are the ones which are contributed by the novice 'Maibi' on the occasion. After a while the 'Pureiromba Laipu' - the person in charge of 'Pureiromba' deity greets the arriving 'Maibis' who are addressed as 'Laiyam'- the deities. Fruits and flowers are offered to the arriving 'Lais' - the deities. In fact this is an act of welcoming the thirteen' Umanglais' by 'Pureiromba'. Next is the preparation for animal sacrifice. The legs of the sacrificial animal is thoroughly washed along with that of the cock. The hog is put on a long banana leaf placing the tip of the leaf facing the shrine. The legs are carefully tied by a rope. In the past the hog was crushed to death by a device made from 'Upan' tree. Now a days the same is killed by hitting on the head. But the cock is simply pressed to death. The hog is pierced by a knife and carefully removed the 'Pei (liver). The 'Pureiromba Laipu' tries to ascertain something by observing the shape, size and position of the 'Pei' (liver) which is known as 'Shapei Yengba'. It will say something about the draught, flood, famine, plentyness of food, diseases and peace and tranquility in the coming months. The 'Laipus' of 'Panam' and 'Chingshomba' also take part in the ritual. After the sacrifice at 'Pureiromba' shrine the hog is brought back to the house of 'Pureiromba Laipu' or the 'Maiba Ahan'.

Now with the completion of the ritual in early morning at the 'Pureiromba' shrine a phase of the celebration is over. However, the much longer part of the celebration which needs a longer preparation is done at the house of 'Pureiromba Laipu'. The main activity is to prepare a feast of Talphut, meat and chicken for offering to deity. The activity here is mainly by women i.e., the 'Maibis'. In some certain areas the participating men help them; for example in roasting the hog, cutting down it into meat meant for cooking, etc. The 'Panam Laipu' and 'Chingshomba Laipu' are the one who are helping in these areas. If necessary the 'Pureiromba Laipu' also reinforces to the above two persons. Another worth mentioning is that the whole activity of cooking and preparing Talphut (roti cooked in boiled water) is not done inside the house but outside the house mostly in the courtyard and at the verandah. So preparation of new hearths are necessary and the same are prepared by the males attending the observation". And hearths are there for cooking the Talphuts, meat and chicken separately. With the exception of the above few areas the celebration may be termed as an all women affair. The Andro society is a male dominated society where women are excluded in most of the rituals and ceremonies. However, in such a male dominated society the women are also given a space to act with a free mind and energy. In fact such a ritual has given the social sanction to the women to drink, dance and to behave according to their wishes but to the extend of their justification during celebration. Again they work with the principle of division of labour. Some of them pound the rice to turn into flour. A few of them paste the flour to make 'Talphut' while two women will boil the 'Talphut' in the boiling water. There in no change in colour in the 'Talphut' before cooking and after. So it is only from the smell that one can ascertain that it is well cooked. However, though the women were given free to act on this day, the cooking of meat is solely the concern of the attending males i.e. the 'Laipus'. The well cooked meat, which is tested by pressing with hands not by tasting, is spread over a broad banana leaf and make it cool down. Like in the same manner the 'Talphut' is also cooked down. From these prepared food sixteen (16) 'Luks' (shared food), one each of Talphut and meat, is arranged in an order for offering to deity. Whatever arranged here at the house of 'Maiba Ahan' i.e. the sixteen 'Luks' are meant for offering here at his residence. Over and above this, a preparation is made for offering to deities located in other areas of the village, i.e., areas around 'Loishang'. For this four small bamboo basket made by bamboo chips; again made by women themselves during the observation itself, is requisitioned. The items to be carried on these four baskets include 'Pangkhok', Yendem (in piece), piece of ginger, dried fish (Ngakha), pieces of 'Khongdrum Khongkha', 'Talphut' and small amount of meat. These four baskets containing the above items and the items meant for 'Loishang' are carried in a march led by 'Maibi Ahan'. Now the baskets are offered one each to the 'Naharup Koso' and 'Ahallup Koso' whereas the remaining two are offered to 'Lamlais' - deities outside the house.

After offering the baskets containing the specified items to the different locations of the deities, now an exchange of foods is carried out between the 'Maibis' and the party of 'Loishang' inside the main shrine of 'Androgee Mei' (Andro fire). During the process of exchange no outsider is allowed to enter the shrine even if one desire to pray it. He will be detained for some time till the handing over is ended. The 'Maibis' submit a small amount of 'Talphut' and meat to the 'Loishang' whereas the 'Loishang' in return hands over the following items to the 'Maibis' which includes (as a token) Chicken, Shingju, Champhut, Ngakha Ngarou (dried fish), Omlet, boiled egg, etc. The Maibis returns to the residence of 'Maibi Ahan' with the foods handed over by 'Loishang' with a message that they can continue their celebration. Now all the sixteen persons including the three 'Laipus' pray to God. Following this the 'Luks' (shared food) are put into their respective baskets by the Maibis. But here they follow their order; the Maibi Ahan leads the collection, followed by 'Maibis' of 'Chingshomba' and 'Panam' etc. The last 'Luk' is the share of the last 'Maibi', the 'Maibi' in the charge of 'Penakhongbi'. The other three 'Luks' are meant for 'Maiba Ahan' and 'Laipus'. The conclusion of the celebration is marked by a feast which always include the 'Yu' (liquor) which is shared equally by both male and female.

F. LANG BAN (AUGUST-SEPTEMBER)[5-6]

I. Lang Ban Chakhangba or Asheeman Khangba

'Langban Chakhangba' or 'Asheeman Khangba' is a ritual performance of death anniversary of deceased person of a family. It is a half month long celebration which begins from the 16th day of 'Langban' (September) and continues till the end of the month. However, it does not mean that a family celebrates the ritual everyday for half a month. But what is practised is to select a convenient day during half a month period. So any family who is having a deceased member has to celebrate the ritual on any convenient day during the half month period.

Lai Barton Touba

A day before the start of 'Langban Chakhangba' a ritual invitation named 'Lai Barton Touba' is held in the night of the full moon day, i.e., on the fifteenth day of 'Langban'. In the past this ritual invitation was held at the depth of night when everybody is in slumber. But now-a-days with the advance of time there is a change in the timing also. People use to perform it early at the dusk in the evening. The ritual invitation is done at the 'Chingkhei' (north–eastern corner) of the courtyard. The place for invitation is cleaned by mopping with water.

Fig. Offering made on the day of 'Langban Chakhangba.'

Fig. Offering of 'Karal' and 'Sharoi Laiyam' at the gate of the house in the ritual 'Langban Chakhangba.'

The offering in the ritual includes fruits, betel nuts & leaves and a light. While offering prayer the person wear a 'Yempak' (a traditional umbrella). The ritual is to invite the deceased father, grandfather, mother, grandmother and as well as the immediate ancestor. Seven generation of father, grandfather, mother, grandmother which are locally described as Parol taret, Purol taret, Emarol taret and Pen lon taret are invited to take part in the celebration. But this mortal being has no power, no way to invite to the soul; so the help of 'Malem Puba Epu Yupanba' is sought. So it is an indirect invitation to the souls through 'Malem Puba Epu Yupanba' deity requesting him to relay the message to the souls at heaven on the 'Langban Chakhangba' to be held in the family. A belief embodied in the ritual invitation is on the duality of home of the soul, the one on the earth and the other in the heaven. After parting the mortal body the soul do not continue to stay on this earth, it will go to the other world; the heaven. The ritual establishes a continues relationship with the souls of the deceased persons in the heaven. But man has no way, no power to invite directly the soul and so seeks the help of the mediator, the 'Malem Puba Epu Yupanba'. Thus the belief says that the souls visit the families on earth at least once a year.

On this occasion 'Luks' (shared meals) including fruits, betel nuts and leaves are offered to the ancestors of seven yeks, nine salais (clans) and to the three Gurus; Mangang, Luwang and Khuman. The prepared 'Luks' are 3,7,9 and it includes the share of the deceased person of the family. The offering compulsorily includes 'Yu' (liquor) without which the celebration is considered imperfect. And both the kinds of 'Yu', i.e. 'Kalei' or 'Haodei' Ayakpa (strong liquor) and 'Wanglei' (Athumba, sweet) are included in the offering. In ritual parlance 'Wanglei' is known as 'Yungou Pumjao'. But in fact this is rice bear.

The ritual offering is held in the verandah at the 'Naktha' side or left side of the verandah of a house facing the east. Whatever offered is placed on trimmed and cut out banana leaves. After offering prayer with the several items offered two persons come out and make a curtain by a white long cloth putting everything offered behind them. And this last for a few. moments. Meaning for this act is that the deities are enjoying the foods offered for them. It is considered unfair to feed the deities in public and hence the curtain hides the activities of the deities on the food.

The offering for 'Karal' and 'Sharoi Laiyam' is made at the gate of the house. The offering for 'Karal' is made for the unnatural cteaths like hanging, drowning, fall from heights and death from lightning, etc. It is a small share for the souls of such unnatural deaths. In the true practice the offering for 'Karal' is to be made in the water; however, it is offered.:on land at the gate.

The offering for 'Sharoi Laiyam' is for the evil spirits like 'Sharoi Ngaroi', etc. A peculiar character on 'Sharoi Laiyam' is to offer anything in parts and pieces. The items offered like flowers, meat, fish and rice etc. are broken into pieces and offered to them for their acceptance. The offering made for 'Karal' and 'Sharoi Laiyam' is done out of fear from their reprisal. Nobody likes to repeat the act of unnatural death in one's family and hence prayed to 'Karal' asking not to re-occur such unwanted unnatural deaths to the family. The 'Sharoi Laiyams' are considered trouble shooters and a prayer to them is a way of asking to free the family from any kind of trouble in future. To make a small share for 'Karal' and 'Sharoi Laiyam' is included in most of the offerings. to other rituals. Even in a small gathering of a few persons the small share of 'Karal' ad 'Sharoi Laiyam' is always included.

When all the offerings have done to all the deities and spirits at different places in and around the house then women of the family perform a short spell of mourning of the deceased person who expired on recent times. Here mourning seems to be the duty of women because not even a single person takes part in it. This short spell of mourning is followed by a feast involving all those present in the occasion. However, cooking and catering of food is marked by the presence of traditional crockery and carriages. For placing the foods banana leaves are used. The rice is carried in a basket (made of bamboo chips) known a 'Thumok' with two handles on opposite sides. The name of this particular basket is 'Pabot Shangbai'. However, the meat and chicken are carried in metal containers like metal bucket and pitcher known as 'Korphu'. Fruits and betel nuts and leaves are placed on broad basket known as 'Shairuk'. Again 'Luks' (shared meal) are prepared for the absentees with any available banana leaves or lotus leaves (Thamna). These 'Luks' are sent to the houses of the absentees by the girls putting them in a basket known as 'Laitang'. Thus 'Langban Chakhangba' concludes with a short prayer and a small feast.

Lam Haiba

This ritual is performed on the first 'Nongmaiching' (Sunday) of 'Langban' (Aug.-Sept.) partly in the precinct of 'Panam Ningthou' and partly at the two extremities of the village known as 'Lamphel Shoi' and "Uran Lakpa'. This is interpreted as a form of 'Langban Chakhangba'at the village level which is held every year as a remembrance of deceased member of a family. However, one finds a remarkable difference on these two observances in many counts. This is also another ritual which is held with the active participation of 'Loishang' - the village authority. The preparation of this occasion is made a few days ahead of the assigned day. The village authority advise the 'Nambors' to let the villagers know that 'Lam Haiba' is being celebrated on the appointed day. Now comes the task of the Nambors to spread the message throughout the length and breadth of the village.

However, they will not go to each and every house of the village but they will execute it with the traditional method of relaying the message known as 'Paothang'. The 'Nambors' at the first instance will give the message to a house nearby the 'Panam Ningthou' - their principal deity. At this instance the task of the 'Nambor' is over and now it is the turn of the family to relay the message to the next house. And the process continues till the last house of the village.

As an .essential part of the observance each and every house has to contribute a certain amount of salt, chilli and 'Yu' (liquor) according to one's capacity. However, the collection of the above items is done a day before the occasion. In the norm of the village a person from a house has to attend the ritual. But this is relaxed to a person who is busy or who is sick.

The celebration of 'LAM HAIBA' is a form of ritual declaration of the ending of monsoon season and heralding of dry season. Monsoon is particularly active in Manipur in June and July and gradually weakened since August. So in the month of September there is opportunity to clean the roads and paths which are filled with grass and leaves during the rainy season. For the convenience of discussion this celebration may be divided into morning part and afternoon part. In the morning around 8 a.m. all the male members of the village assemble in the ground of 'Panam Ningthou'. Those assembled is divided into two groups namely, 1. Ahallup Pana and 2. Naharup Pana where 'Panas' is an administrative unit. In 'Andro' all the lineages belong to either of the two 'Panas' for their village administration: The morning ritual is performed in the two 'Pana Shang' (Pana house) located near the 'Shang len' (main house) of 'Panam Ningthou' which is on the other side of the road. So the villagers belonging to either of the two 'Panas' assemble again in their respective 'Pana Shang' (Pana house) for the conduct of the ritual. There are places for four deities in each of the 'Pana Shang' i.e. 1).

Loumilakpa 2). Loumihidang, 3). Khabam Lakpa and 4). Khabam Hidang.

The morning part ends with a brief prayer to these deities begging for a healthy and wealthy village. The prayer includes the offering of sweets and fruits in the 'Laibung' - the altar. Those assembled in the morning which even includes the old persons parted from the 'Pana Shang' after sharing a small amount of 'Shingju' of 'Ushoi' (bamboo shoots). However, women are excluded from such gathering and it is perfectly a male affair.

The afternoon part of the celebration begins around 2 p.m. with the gathering of all the male members of the village in the ground of 'Panam Ningthou'. Once again those gathered is broadly divided into two groups but not in the line of 'Pana' division; one group led by Khullakpa, Pakhanglakpa and Nahallakpa and the other group led by 'Khunjahanba'. Both the groups will go to the extreme ends of the village in the east and in west in a procession which also include old persons. The group led by 'Khullakpa' goes to the east to the extreme end of the village named 'Lamphel Shoi'. The other led by 'Khunjahanba' will go to the west to the extreme end of the village named "Uran Lakpa'.

The procession is led by a 'Khangjeng' (a bachelor) with a Thangjou (dagger) in his hand who occasionally slash tall grass and shrubs on their way- from which act the name 'Lam Haiba' is derived. The procession includes 'Pung' (drum) and 'Shel' (dish). It passes Sanapat Leikai and finally reaches 'Lamphel Shoi' which is around 5 kms. away from proper Andro. All along the way they beat the drum and 'shel' in the tune 'Chong Tring', 'Chong Khrap'. The beating of the drum and 'Shel' is the task of the 'Khangjengs' (bachelors). Here at 'Lamphel Shoi' offering is made to deity with a sacred fire from the traditional source of fire,- 'Maiba Chingba'. The offering include 'Yu' (liquor),'rice, Shingju, Champhut and a cooked chicken besides flowers available on the spot of the ritual. A similar offering is also done on the western extremity of the village. 'Lam Haiba' is also known as 'Langban Ukrong Hongba'. The purpose of this .ritual is to pray to God for a healthy and productive year. After the prayer the chicken is shared among the 'Khangjengs' and married persons cannot take part in it. However, the 'Yu' (liquor) is shared among them irrespective of their age. At the fag end of the ritual an item known as 'Lei Langba' is held where the 'Khangjengs' are assigned to collect lotus flower from the nearby lake. The procession return with the flowers only to be submitted to the 'Loishang' signifying that they have performed the ritual. But for the west they return with a green leaf and submit it to the authority as a token that they have also conducted the ritual successfully. Both the groups arrive at a ground known as 'Panthong Lampak' ; this time not in the 'Panam' ground. Here it is a huge gathering including children, Khangjengs, adults and old persons. The day long ceremony concludes with the sharing of 'Shingju' and 'Yu' (liquor) by all those gathered in the ground.

G. MERA (SEPTEMBER-OCTOBER)[7]

1. Kurak Lamtaiba

It is a ritual held on the first 'Erai' of 'Mera' (Sept. - Oct.) month i.e. on the first 'Friday' of the month. This ritual is held at a time when the rainy season is almost closing and the people are preparing for harvest. In other areas of Manipur the ritual is held in the beginning of rainy season. The ritual is found prevalent in many rural areas of Manipur. However 'Kurak Lamtaiba' in 'Andro' is found to be different from other areas of Manipur in aspects like timing, ingredients in ritual, etc. 'Kurak Lamtaiba' seems to be a transformation from the term 'Kumlak Lamtaiba' meaning the bordering of two seasons. In fact this is a ritual held at the border of autumn season and winter season.

Fig. Offering made on the ritual 'Kurak Lamtaiba.'

The ritual is held at the border of the village located on a hillock in the direction 'Santhong' (south-west) of the village. A brief preparation for the ritual is made a few days ahead of the designated day. Items like rice, salt, chilli, etc. are collected from each and every house where one has to contribute to one's capacity. There is no fix amount of subscription. However, 'Waiyu' (rice bear) is to be prepared by a few selected houses where the selection is the task of the 'Loishang'. These selected houses will not engage in preparing 'Waiyu' for the next year where the task is assigned to some other houses. So the return of the turn takes many years as the village is a big one. The ritual is held in the morning before noon. The afternoon part is mostly the gathering of elders of the village. Children also attend the gathering in large numbers. But women are excluded from the ritual. The ritual include the sacrifice of a chicken and the same is subscribed by 'Khullakpa' and 'Luplakpa' every year. In the past a person from the 'Kabui' tribe was invited in the ritual. He was entertained in the aftermath of the ritual. He was allowed to carry away the pitchers which are utilised in the ritual. But in these days the practice is no longer prevalent.

While performing the ritual the 'Pujaris' of the village (from pujari Loishang) cooks the subscribed material like rice, etc. And the curry is one item only and this is 'Yen Chagem Pomba' - boiling the chicken in rice. Here we find a division of labour where a few 'Pujaris' are engaged in cooking while a few others are engaged in fetching water from the nearby pond. Meanwhile the 'Waiyu' (rice bear) which are put in large jars are drained to mugs by means of pipes. This 'Waiyu' is treated to everybody present in the occasion at intervals before serving the 'Yen Chagem Pomba'.

The site of the ritual. which has been performing since the last many centuries is located on a near plane hillock. The ground is almost plane and is thoroughly cleaned. At the centre of the ground a pole named 'Kabak' is erected. This pole is around 8 ft. in height. It is made from the stem of 'Heimang' tree. The stem is thoroughly peeled and while doing so it is radiating its whitish colour. On the tip of the post seven other pieces of the tree which are cut in unequal lengths are inserted; the longest at the bottom and the shortest at the top of all. However, the cut pieces are arranged in symmetrical manner, the shortest at the top is followed by longer ones till the longest at the bottom. The research needs to answer the significance of this cultural symbol. It seems to be a prayer to the rain god for no rain during the ensuing harvesting season.

The using of such pole in rituals in found in some of the hill tribes of Manipur which is particularly true of the Maring tribe. It seems to be a replacement of animal sacrifice which was popular at one time. The sacrificed animal was kept hanging at the pole. Now it seems the 'Kabak' replaces the sacrificed animal. Rice is harvested early in the hills, earlier than valley which is activated only since November. But in the hills October is opportune time for harvesting. At one time the Andros also settled in the hills. It seems to be a matter of accompanying their tradition in the hills to this village at the foot of 'Nongmaiching' hill. Again the site of the ritual on a small hillock substantiate the above theory of animal sacrifice.

At the concluding part of the ritual the cooked rice is carefully observed by the elders of the village so as to predict something relating to rain, diseases, etc. After a short prayer for good harvest and a village free from diseases etc. the cooked food is served to all those assembled there and the feast is enjoyed by everyone there.

Leichreng Leitaba

It is another ritual performed in the month 'Mera'. This ritual is connected with the collection of 'Leichreng' (coarse soil) from the hillock named 'Champra Chingdong' which is a component raw material for pottery. This is discussed in detail at another chapter on pottery.

H. HIYANGGEI (OCTOBER - NOVEMBER)[8]

i. Ningol Chakouba

This festival, which is an extended festival from the Meiteis, is held on the second day of 'Hiyanggei' (Oct. - Nov.) month every year. The festival is simple; the married daughters are invited by the parents or brothers for a feast of a variety of dishes prepared out of the vegetables and fishes available during the season. The daughters visits their parental home with an 'Athenpot' including 'Yu'. The 'Athenpot' includes mostly sweets, fruits, betel nuts and leaves, etc. She will serve the 'Yu' (liquor) to her father and brothers. However, she will carry away the left over 'Yu' when she return to her home. She comes back after showering blessing to her brothers.

REFERENCES

1. Oral interview with Ch. Kumar and Ch. Palandro of Andro Khunou Leikai.
2. Corroborated by physical participation.
3. Oral interview with Ph. Tonjao and Ch. Thambal.
4. Oral interview with Sarungbam Kullachandra, 'Maiba Ahan' of Andro Khunou Leikai and Corroborated by physical participation.
5. Oral interview with Ch. Palandro of Khunou Leikai, Andro.
6. Oral interview with Ch. Surchandra of Sanapat Leikai, Andro. & Corroborated by physical participation.
7. Oral interview with S. Lalito, Y. Umachandra and H. Hemlet and supported by physical participation.
8. Prepared in consultation with Ningthoujam Shyam of Andro Mamang Leikai.

11

MAIN FESTIVALS PANAM HARAOBA AND PUREIROMBA HARAOBA

ACCOUNT OF PANAM

Like the Meiteis the Andros also worship 'Umaglais' (sylvan deities); however they worship only thirteen (13) 'Umanglais' where the Meiteis worship as many as 363 Umanglais. For the Andros 'Pureiromba' ranks first in the order of Umanglais, followed by 'Chingshomba' and 'Panam'. However due reverence is given to 'Panam' and even upgraded to 'Lainingthou' (king of gods or supreme god). In the event of 'Panam Haraoba' festival any outsider is not allowed to enter, stay or trespass the village. Local volunteers are engaged for the strict implementation of the custom. So the Andros have established an aura around 'Panam' so as to distinguish themselves from others. But the oral tradition reveal that the 'Panam' is closely allied to 'Angom Salai' (clan). The tradition says the 'Panam' is not the original name, and the earlier name is 'Nam Shababa', brother of 'Nam Shathiba' (Nongpok Ningthou). And 'Shelloi Langmai' is also not the birth place of 'Panam'. 'Shelloi Langmai' is the birth place of his wife 'Sabon Yairel'. The birth place of 'Panam' is 'Huikap Maning Ching', a southern range of 'Nongmaiching' hill. A tragic incident on his life forced him to shift from 'Huikap Maning Ching' to Shelloi Langmai'. One day 'Nam Shathiba

(Nongpok) attempted the life of 'Nam Shababa' (Panam) with a spear. 'Nam Shababa' was fatally wounded and was on the verge of death. But it was his dog who helped to save his life. The dog snatched the blood stained 'Khudei' (loin cloth) around his neck and presented to his wife. The dog bite her cloth and dragged toward her injured husband. In this way his wife saved 'Panam'. From this incident his wife persuaded him to shift to 'Shelloi Langmai', her ancestral home. From the incident onward 'Panam' stayed on 'Shelloi Langmai' till his death.

At present a small grove is kept reserved on the outskirts of the village adjoining the hill. But the shrine is located in the village in the 'Andro Awang Leikai'. It is near the 'Androgi Mei' (the Andro fire), and on the northern side of the road passing at the heart of the village. The 'Panam Laipu', the person in charge of the deity, looks after the shrine. The shrine is opened only on Sunday. So people offer prayer on Sunday with offerings containing coins, 'Kabok' (puffed rice), fruits etc. Anyone who comes other than Sunday offer prayer outside the shrine.

An annual offering at the village level is held in the month of 'Lamta' (February-March) on the first 'Thangja' (Saturday) which is known as 'Sharen Chanba'. The animal sacrificed is a pig. And the tradition continues without any break. The offering last the whole day, beginning from morning till dark, although the animal sacrifice is held in the morning. The seven members of the 'Loishang' (Village authority), sixteen (16) members, eight (8) each from 'Ahallup' and 'Naharup Pana' and the elders of the village attend the ritual. However, women are excluded from the ritual. It is mainly a business of manfolk. Subsequent to this offering the 'Panam Haraoba' festival is held for five days. However, it does not meant that 'Haraoba' festival is held every year after this ritual. Instead there is circumstance which leads to the festival.

A BRIEF ACCOUNT OF PANAM HARAOBA

'Haraoba' may be interpreted as a festival of pleasing god. The account of 'Panam Haraoba' is very brief. This festival is very exclusive and as a result no outsider is allowed to participate in the festival. He or she cannot stay nor trespass the village during the period of 'Haraoba'. This is true even in collecting information on the festival. So the account is sketchy, however; the following is a humble attempt on the festival. In the tradition of this village the 'Haraoba' festival is held only when the shrine of the deity is fallen to the ground due to old age. Following this a new shrine is constructed and the same is inaugurated after placing the deity in the new house. This is known as 'Shangkaba' in the local parlance. The inauguration of the shrine is followed by 'Haraoba' festival which last for five days. Then this is held in the month of Lamta (February-March). And this is followed by 'Pureiromba Haraoba' in 'Kalen' (April-May). If 'Haraoba' festival 'is held this year then it is definitely followed in the next year. In the next year the festival is held with a new name of 'Chaoren Haraoba' which last for nine days.

In the next year the festival is held in the same month 'L.amta' (February-March). In the case of 'Panam Haraoba' there is no incident of 'Lai Ekouba' - an act of invoking the deity from water. Instead the deity is moved out from the grove in the foothill a day before the festival. The 'Panam Laipu' - the person in charge of the deity proceed to the grove at the depth of night. He is alone and no one is accompanied with him. He is not allowed to carry a light even. Again no one is allowed to witness the action of the 'Panam Laipu'. In this way he alone moves out the deity from the grove to his house. The night is spent at the house of the 'Laipu'. This 'Laipu' is hereditary and their lineage is in charge of the deity since the ancient days. With the news of the deity having moved out from the grove the 'Khangjengs' (the bachelors, the youths) approaches the 'Laipu' to handover the deity to the community to perform the 'Haraoba' festival. The request is readily agreed by the 'Laipu' and thus handover the deity to them. However at this stage the elders of the village appear in the scene. The elders like 'Loumilakpa', 'Loumihidang', etc. take the responsibility of carrying the deity on a chariot from the house of the 'Laipu' to 'Laipung' - the ground of Andro fire. On the first day of the festival an elaborate offering including flowers, fruits, chickens, animals, etc. is held. The ritual 'Sharen Chanba'.where the animal is sacrificed - is held on the opening day. The sacrificed animal is cooked and a feast is held where all those present including the seven officials take part in the feast. On this opening day dances are also held, however, in brief. In the night the 'Khong Shuba' - the ritual drumming is performed. In fact this is an act of pounding on a pestle made from a dug-out by mortars of wood. It produces a peculiar sound. In the morning of next days the 'Lai Yakaiba' - the ceremonial awakening of the deity is performed. The instrument used is a small drum known as 'Lamtai Pung'. Flowers are also offered. The 'Panas' also perform their duties. The girls who are known as 'Ningol Macha' also take part in the festival. They will come out after taking their evening meal which they term as 'Chakum-Chaka'. And they eventually take part in the ritual dance named as 'Humai Chongba'. The dance sequence known as "Lere Jagoi" is excluded in 'Panam Haraoba' festival.

'Ngaprum Kappa' - the ritual shooting of an Eel fish is common to both the 'Panam' and 'Pureiromba Haraoba' festival. For this the actor uses catapult and an arrow where he aims to the items like flowers, fruits etc. and to all those present including the officials of 'Loishang.' And he collects the items he touches to his 'Tungol' - a basket use in collecting fish while fishing with a fishnet in particular where the basket fastened at the waist of the person. If someone fails to offer in kind can do so in cash or coin. *It is somewhat similar with*

'Naka Thengba' where children visits houses and beg *for kind or cash during the 'Yaoshang' festival.* On the concluding day of 'Chaoren Houba' an sporting event is included where a race is held among the youths. It is matter of long distance running, where the strongest person is selected full view of the public. The festival concludes with the ritual 'Agar Hangen-Meckon Thagonba'. Laibungthou Mapan'- the nine office beares who are in charge of nine different deities sings song in praise of Ebuthou' - the Lord.

PUREIROMBA HARAOBA

'Pureiromba Haraoba' is held in the month of 'Kalen' (April -May). The festival is held in the precinct of 'Pureiromba' shrine. In maximum the festival last for twelve days. And the duration varies from year to year. The festival may last for five or six days in the minimum depending upon the nature of the year. The duration of the festival is decided by an astrologer by observing the nature of the year which, in their jargon is known as 'Laichan Yengba'. The account of 'Pureiromba Haraoba' is more sketchy even though the festival is open to outsider. The festival has not been held for the past many year and as a result of this there is no chance to witness such a festival. However, the following is a short account of the festival. The festival begins with the ritual 'Lai Ekouba' in which the deity is awakened by invoking from water. Later the deity is believed to be placed in the shrine. It is the 'Maibi' (priestess) who perform the ritual'Lai Ekouba' and no other person can do it. This 'Lai Ekouba' is followed by 'Lei Langba' - floral offering by 'Laroi' group of 'Khangjengs' where 'Khangjengs' are the bachelors. 'Laroi' is the group of youths whose task is to collect 'La' (banana leaf) from the banana groves of the village. Besides there are other 'Lois' depending upon the nature of task. The major participants in 'Pureiromba' festival are women. And they are mostly the thirteen 'Maibis' (priestess) of the thirteen

'Umanglais'. The dance sequence is as follows - (i) Khubak Yeinaba, (ii) Laibou Macha, (iii) Humai Chongba, (iv) Lou Yanba, (v) Fibul Lokpa, (vi) Leishem Jagoi - this sequence is performed by 'Ningol Macha' - the girls, (vii) Ngaprum Kappa - as mentioned earlier it is an act of shooting the Eel by an arrow using a catapult, (viii) 'Lere Jagoi' - this has been transformed from the name 'Leire Jagoi'. The festival ends with the dance 'Laibou Achouba'. The concluding part is similar with 'Panam Haraoba' festival. In this also the ritual 'Agar Hangen' - Meekon Thagonba' is performed where the 'Laibungthou Mapan' - the nine office bearers who are in charge of nine different deities sing song in praise of ' Ebuthou' - the Lord.

A dance sequence in 'Pureiromba Haraoba' festival (a demonstration)

REFERENCE

Prepared in consultation with Ph. Achou of Andro Mamang Leikai. and Y. Dharmo, former Khullakpa of Andro.

12

LOISHANG AS POLITY

'Loishang' is the village authority of Andro. This is manned by seven officials where 'Khullakpa' is the village chief. He works along with other six officials who are 'Luplakpa', 'Khunjahanba', 'Khabamlakpa', 'Yupanba', 'Pakhanglakpa' and 'Nahalakpa'. The 'Loishang' do not have the power to frame laws but they have the right to enforce their customary laws. In such a situation they exercise judiciary power to some extent. But in the past when Manipur was under Kingship their judgement was the final. They are the custodian of customs and traditions of the Andros. This 'Loishang' is assisted by four 'Nambors' who are appointed by the village authority. They are the one who perform the orderly works of the 'Loishang'.

In the past in the days of Kingship it was the king who appointed the 'Khullakpa' and his six officials. The appointment was effected by the issuing of an edict. However, a proposal from the village for their appointment precedes the edict of the king. Till date there is no fix tenure for the 'Khullakpa' and his six officials. They will be in office as long as their service is satisfactory to the villagers. It is the village who appoints a 'Khullakpa', but at the same time as a prerogative he is given the right to select his officials by himself or in consultation with the village elders. With the replacement of Kingship by democracy it is the villagers who appoints the 'Khullakpa' and his officials. Again it is the villagers who can remove the officials in masse if the necessary arises. So the sovereign power rest on the villagers. Very recently in and around March and April, 2006 there was an incident of replacing all the seven officials in masse by a new one after the former was found involved in a serious scandal which is detrimental to the age old custom of the Andros. But in the event of retiring from 'Khullakpa' he also has to handover the Copper plate to incoming 'Khullakpa'. It was king 'Punshiba' who offered a copper plate to the 'Khullakpa' of Andro. Significantly it was king 'Punshiba' (1404 - 1432 A.D.) who declared the boundary of the Andro Village along with a tax free land.

ISSUES SETTLED BY LOISHANG

The 'Loishang' bears the responsibility to settle various issues which arises among the villagers ranging from thefts, divorce and eloping etc. In such cases it is the 'Luplakpa' who plays the role of an advocate. He will admit the appeal of a person or persons of opposing sides and will place it over the table of 'Loishang'. 'Khullakpa' will preside over the hearing of the case. It is the seven officials who will take the decision.

A lengthy debate prevails before coming to a unanimous decision. If the decision is beyond someone's satisfaction then he is given the right to appeal to a court. Again if the person fails to achieve a favourable judgement from the court then he has to face double punishment both from the court as well as from 'Loishang'. Here the 'Loishang' executes the punishment in stages. First he will get punishment in the form of fine. If he accept the punishment and pays fine to the village then the action of the 'Loishang' ends here. Instead if the person shows disregard of the punishment, then the 'Loishang', as a last resort will expel the person from the village. But here the person is not physically removed from the village, what is actually done is to remove him from the 'Pana' administration. The 'Loishang' issues notices to the villagers to disassociate the person in the event of functions like marriage, death ceremony, etc. The 'Pujaris' and 'Arangbas' are also advised not to help the person. In the aftermath of such a proclamation the elders of the village will avoid the family in any social function. However, his close relatives including his brothers and sisters do not come under the purview of such a proclamation. And they are allowed to associate with the person in any social function. There is no fix period for the expulsion. And there is no variation in period in the expulsion depending upon the variety of the case. There is no difference in treatment on cases pertaining to theft, kidnapping of a girl, etc. Once he is expelled, he is expelled for forever. However, after a few days of his expulsion he can make an appeal to the 'Loishang' to pardon his wrongdoing. Subsequently the village authority can review their former decision and can bring the erring person to the 'Pana' administration. But he cannot escape the punitive action of the authority and he will be fined a sum of Rs. 1000/- which is known as 'Wakongba' in the local parlance. The amount can be bargained and accordingly the burden is relaxed to some extent. In the past when money economy was not in sight the fine might be in the form of kind. And the items might be a pig and 'Yu' (liquor). The amount Rs. 1000/- is utilised as fees for the office bearers and in treating the elders who are present in the occasion. A person cannot escape such punitive action even if the authority forgives him after two or three years of the expulsion. Expulsion is a painful punishment in Andro. Because it is a community based society. It is the community who helps a family in executing social functions like marriage, death ceremony; Langban Chakhangba; etc. The community helps in collecting banana leaves, fire wood, water, etc.

Without the community the family has to execute all these things which certainly is a big burden to them.

NAMBORS (A STAFF OF LOISHANG)

The 'Loishang' runs its administration with a small staff known as Nambors. It is four in number. They are appointed by the 'Loishang'. They are also known as 'Khagemba Loishang'. The 'Loishang' can remove anyone from among them if he is found suffering from poor performance. In the event of any vacancy the 'Loishang' issues a notice for recruitment and applications are invited from intending candidates. If the applicants are more than one then the 'Loishang' has the sole right to select the best person for the post. There is no fix tenure for the post and one can serve'as long as he desires. He can resign from the post when he feels to do so as compelled by unavoidable circumstances. As a routine work the four 'Nambors' clean and sweep the precinct of 'Loishang' everyday. They will also run for errands informing the villager of rites and rituals, like 'Kurak Lamtaiba', etc. They will also run for message in the events like fire in the village, etc. However, he has not to run through the length and breath of the village. Instead he works on a certain modus operandi. There are certain houses for giving a message. His task is to relay the message to such a nearby house. The house in turn relay the news to the next house and the process continues till the last house. If anyone fails in such a message he will be punished by a fine of Rs. 50/-.

REFERENCES

1. Oral interview with Ph. Achou of Andro Mamang Leikai.
2. Oral interview with Ph. Gopal of Andro Khunou Leikai.

13

LOISHANG AS FOUNTAINHEAD OF CUSTOM AND RITES

As mentioned in the previous chapter 'Loishang' is the overall authority of the village as regard the enforcing of customs and traditions. Their authority is more pronounced in executing the calendar of rites and rituals in the village. In fact their involvement is found in almost all the rites and rituals which are community based. However, customs and traditions like 'Hiru Kaba', Androgi Mei (Fire worship), 'Thashi Numitki Lai Khurumba', etc. survives under direct supervision of Loishang. The following discussion highlights the extent of the hold of 'Loishang' in customs and traditions specially in the above rites and customs.

1. Officals of Loishang

The seven officials of 'Loishang' are as follows: (i) Khullakpa, (ii) Luklakpa, (iii) Khunjahanba, (iv) Khabam Lakpa, (v) Yupanba, (vi) Pakhanglakpa and (vii) Naharakpa who are supervising the entire rites and rituals of the community with a spirit to safeguard the age old custom and tradition have their responsibility of taking in charge of seven different deities who are signified as 'Pung'.

(i) Khullakpa

The name of 'Laipham Pung' is 'Chingu Paothempung'. 'Punglen' - the supreme 'Pung' is the embodiment of daylight the 'Anganba'. The 'Laipham Pana' of 'Yaiskul' is coronated by the deity 'Pakhangba'. Its coronation name is 'Moishit'. It is also known as 'Langyen Shal'.

It is about ascending the throne by 'Thangjing Gurushidaba'. It is the secret account of the 17 deities of Thangjing. 'Pakhangba' ruled for two chaks (eras). Khullakpa is in charge of this 'Laiphampung'.

(ii) Luklakpa

The name of 'Meipung' is 'Thangji Upi Urenpung'. This 'Punglen' is the destiny of mankind in their birth, living and in death. The deity Lainingthou Pakhangba' associates with it. It is all about the coronation of 'Chingu Nongthou Sorarel'. Luklakpa is in charge of this 'Pung'.

(iii) Khunjahanba

The name of 'Tingshang pung' is Khomlen Leima Paothempung'.

This 'punglen' signifies the sight, slumber and the awakening of mankind. 'Nongpok Achiba' is in charge of 'Khurai' and the coronation seat is in 'Khurai'. It is all about the coronation of 'Chingkhei Guru Shidaba'. It happens in 'Pakhangba era'. 'Khunjahanba' is in charge of 'Naharup Pana Sebok Pala Pung'.

(iv) Khabam Lakpa

The 'Pung' of 'Khabam' is Tanbamikap-Pung'. It signifies the beginning and ending of rainy season which says 'Enga Kumdamba' and 'Engel Kumkhaiba'. It is all about the coronation of 'Pakhangba' on 'Leipak Chaba Pana Ariba Pala Khurai'.

The coronation name is 'Muba Kaoyai Toppa'. It associates with seven streams and hence the name 'Nikba Kaoyai Thangba'. It is about the coronation of 'Koubru Achiba'. It is the 'Pakhangba' of the first 'Chak' (era). It is the name of the deity who associates with 'Khawai'. 'Khabam Lakpa' is in charge of 'Nongchup Leipak Chaba Pala Khabam Pana'.

(v) Yupanba

The name of 'Yupung' is 'Thingkam Pung'. This 'Punglen' signifies the all living beings on the earth with their regular pulses. The deity 'Pakhangba' ascends the throne on 'Wangkhei Pana'. Its coronation name is 'Ngangba Kao Chihenba'. It is all about the coronation of 'Wangbren'. 'Pakhangba' reigns for four chaks. The duty of 'Pana is done first by Hanana. Feeding of rice is first by 'Laipham'. It was the tradition. Yupanba is in charge of 'Ahallup Pana Naha Pakhangba of four chaks.

(vi) Pakhanglakpa

The name of 'Khongpung' is 'Taibang Shaktakpung'. This 'Punglen' signifies that Korou (Sun) was once near the earth. Further it says that 'Korou' (sun) is the father and 'Malem' (earth) is the mother of mankind. This 'pung' is associated with deity 'Pakhangba'. It is all about the coronation of 'Panthou Guru Shidaba', the almighty. Pakhanglakpa is in charge of this 'Pung'.

(vii) Naharakpa

The name of 'Erep-phu Pung' is 'Shuta Shoitapung'. This 'Punglen' signifies that the progenitors begets its siblings and thus spreads the world over. It also enlightens the world from its mental darkness. It is all about the coronation of 'Palem Ema Leiphurel Namungbi Nongphuren Achipi'. Naharakpa is in charge of this 'Pung'.

2. HIRU KABA (LAISHANA KANA FAMDAMBA)

In Andro the life of a person is divided into different stages and each stage is assigned a definite task or fitted to an organisation. 'Hiru Kaba' is one among them and this is

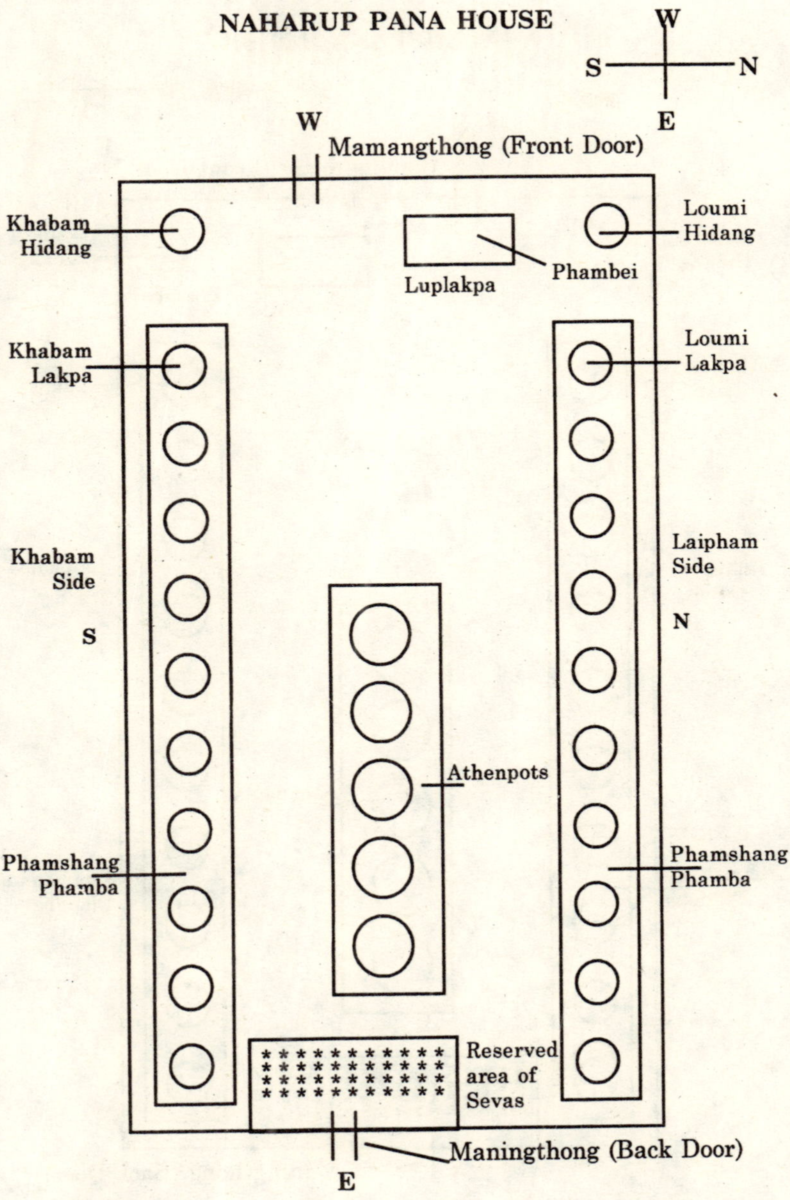

Sitting arrangement in Naharup Pana House in 'Hiru Kaba' ritual.

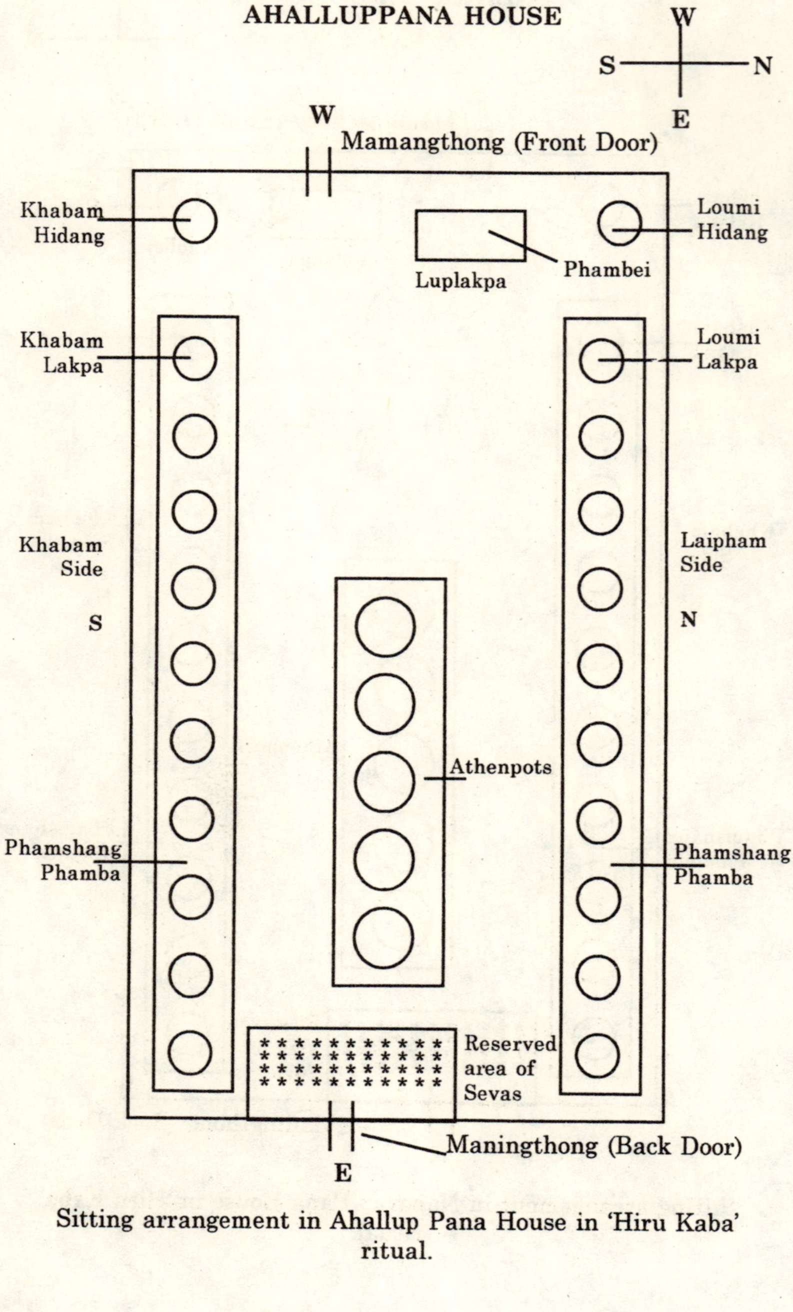

Sitting arrangement in Ahallup Pana House in 'Hiru Kaba' ritual.

performed only when he is admitted as a member of 'Pana' division where there are two (open) Panas. Besides there are two more Panas in secret and they are 'Londumba' and 'Keidila'. As compelled by tradition a person on completion of six months after his marriage he has to become a member of the 'Pana' division.

The admission into 'Pana' is known as 'Loumi Thouba' where the person will expend a chicken and a bottle of 'Yu' (liquor). Now in place of 'Yu' a sum of Rs. 201- is charged. So after clearing his fees he is entitled to serve in the 'Loishang'. He will remain as 'Seva' for a few months. He is now entitled to take part in the prayer service of the four deities. And he will remain so for at least one and half a month duration. However, the months 'Wakching' (January), 'Shachiphu' (April) and 'Thawan' (August) are considered as polluted months. And the ceremony 'Hiru Kaba' cannot be held on these months. So after passing one and half a month or more the ceremony 'Hiru Kaba' is held in the Pana Shang' (Pana house). It is held in the morning. The required ingredients are (a) seven hands of banana, (b) puffed rice, (c) betel nuts and leaves, (d) sweet smelling fruits, (e) 'Shingju; and (f) 'Waiyu' (rice bear). On this occasion an official, either the 'Khullakpa' (village chief) or 'Luplakpa', will take part as presiding authority. For 'Ahallup Pana; the 'Khullakpa' presides the ceremony. In case of 'Naharup Pana' the 'Luplakpa' takes the chair. And their seat is known as 'Phambei'. The face of 'Pana Shang' (Pana house) faces west, and so the main door is in the west. Although there is a small door also in the east which is treated as the back of the house. The main door is in the centre of the house. The sitting arrangement is such that the 'Khullakpa' sits at the right side near the door. The deity 'Loumihidang' is located at the right corner (north-western corner), And the deitv 'Khabam Hidang' is located at south-western corner of the house, i.e. on the left corner. Then comes the rows of 'Phamshang

Phamba'. They sit in two rows facing each other. Their rows runs west to east. Again in each row there are ten persons. They are all who have performed 'Hirukaba' ritual. The sitting arrangement is in order of seniority. And the seniormost sits at the front. In the centre of the room 'Athenpots' are kept. In the eastern side of the house, around the smaller eastern door, the six 'Loumi Thouba' make their presence. Here they are termed as 'Seba Changba' party. They will do here orderly works and their service is supervised by those on the 'Phamshang Phamba'. The two rows of 'Phamshang Phamba' are given names; the one on the right side is 'Laipham' and the other on the left side is 'Khabam'. In this way by a simple ceremony the ritual 'Hirukaba' is performed. However, the ceremony includes the offer of gold and silver which is termed as "Sana Lupa Konyai Hunba". At the end of the gathering they enjoy the taste of 'Singju'; a kind of raw vegetables palao.

There are stages in the life of a person while he is in the 'Pana'. He enters the 'Pana; as "Loumi Thouba'. He will remain as 'Seva' till he performs 'Hirukaba'. 'Hirukaba' is a form of promotion, promoting someone to a fulfledged 'Pana' member. But the last rite which one has to perform in. his 'Pana' life is 'Famchak Chaba'. In this ritual it involves a small feast. Even after performing 'Famchak Chaba' he will continue to remain in the 'Pana' with new assignments and responsibilities till his health permits. He gets new assignments in the ritual and ceremonies like 'Kurak Lamtaiba', 'Lamta Thangja' and 'Lam Haiba' etc. He will participate in the collection of rice from house to house, banana leaves from forest and in the collection of firewood, etc. He will also take part in cooking in the rituals and ceremonies. Besides the collection of necessary items for rituals and ceremonies from houses of the village is also his responsibility. However,' the elderly persons who are taking part in the Kurak Lamtaiba' ritual are exempted from such duties and responsibilities. So one has to perform the above duties till he reaches the age of the above described elderly persons.

3. THASHI NUMITKI LAI KHURUMBA

This is an occasion of worshipping the 'Panam Ningthou' - their principal deity once in a month. The day is on the last day of a month of lunar calendar. The day is known as 'Thashi', whose literal meaning is dead month. On this day one cannot see the moon in the night sky and hence counted that the moon is dead. And so the name 'Thashi' for this night. On every 'Thashi' the 'Panam Ningthou' is worshipped. Worshipping of 'Panam' on this day was an event which involved the whole village. With the advance of time the village becomes larger and celebration became hard to manage. So the seven officials of 'Loishang' worshipped 'Panam' in representation of the village. The worshipping is held in the morning around 8/9 a.m. The necessary items for the worshipping like fruits, flowers, 'Yu' (liquor), cooked fish and meat and rice, etc. are contributed by eight houses. The above items are offered to their principal deity and prayed. After the prayer the offered items are enjoyed by the seven official along with the attending eight persons. Entertaining of one or two guests is also allowed. The same items are contributed by another eight houses for the next 'Thashi'. The preparation of roster of eight houses is the responsibility of the 'Loishang'. The first batch of eight houses begins from the houses nearby the Loishang. This first batch communicates to another eight houses for the next 'Thashi'. And the process continues in this manner till the last eight houses. As the village is big enough.the return of the first batch take more than four years.

SANGLEN (MAIN HOUSE)

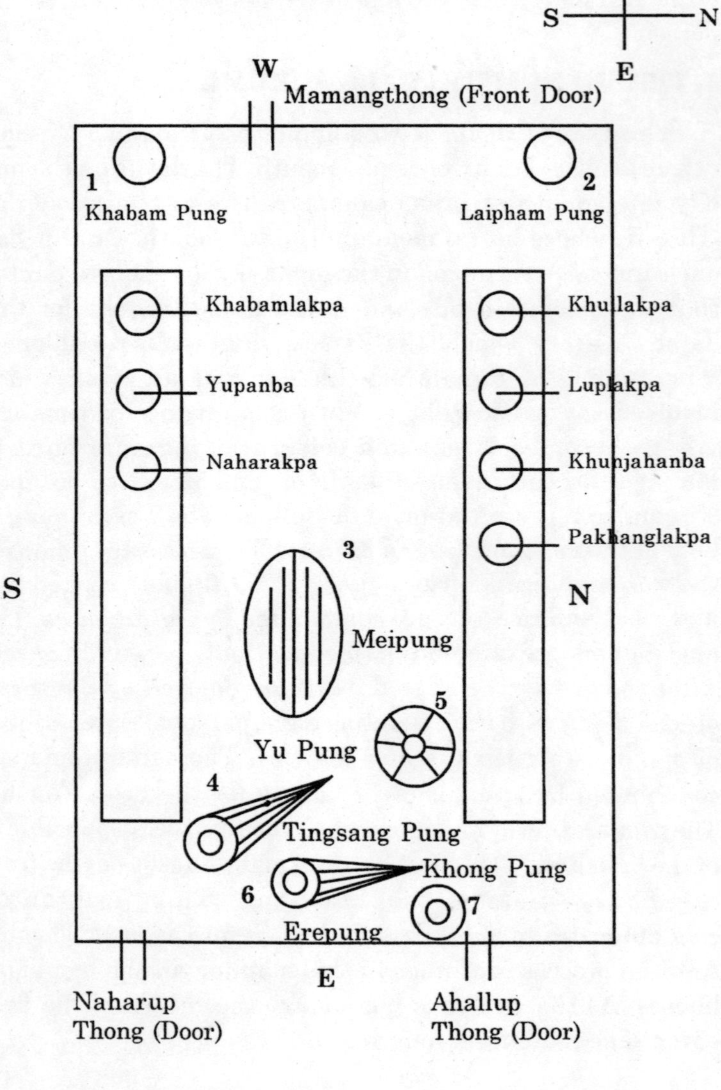

The position of the seven 'Pungs' and the seven office bearers of 'Loishang' in the Shanglen (Main House) where the Androgi Mei (the sacred fire) is housed.

4. ANDROGI MEI (ANDRO FIRE)

Among the living traditions in Andro the fire worship is worthwhile. And this fire is famous as 'Androgi Mei' (the Andro fire). It is a popular belief among the Andro that this fire was accompanied by 'Poireiton', the wanderer, who wandered from place to place in search of a suitable habitable place. And this occured during the reign of King Nongda Lairen Pakhangba (34 A.D.-154 A.D;) of Manipur. Afterwards the fire was venerated by the people of this region and subsequently deified. It was king 'Punshiba' (1404 A.D.-1432 A.D.) who declared a large tract of forest in 'Nongmaiching' hill reserved for the fire deity. The fire is often described as "Upi Urep Chaba Laì" - meaning a deity who eats firewoods. Besides Andro, the people around Andro village and beyond consider this fire as a sacred one. Still it is a regular feature to collect fire from Andro by the people of Manipur in the event of opening ceremony of annual sports of a club or any important 'function involving fire worship. As an institution, this fire is under the supervision of 'Nambors' - the persons appointed by village authority, the 'Loishang', to look after especially the 'Panam' and its surroundings. For this, in rotation, a pair of two houses each in the village will be in charge of the fire for everyday. However, the return of the turn takes a long time as the village is a big one. The 'Nambors' are empowered to punish anybody found dereliction in one's duty. Even if the person fails to obey the 'Nambors' at this stage the matter is referred to 'Loishang'. And the matter further complicates. The sole reason for all these is the strong reverence to the fire which they consider any break in the fire would lead to misfortune in the village.

REFERENCES

1. Oral interview with Ph. Achou of Andro Mamang Leikai.
2. Oral interview with Heikhrujam Mohon Singh of Andro Machengpat Leikai.

3. Oral interview with Ch. Palandro of Andro Khunou Leikai.
4. Oral interview with N. Shyam of Andro Mamang Leikai.

14

BACKGROUND OF PLACE NAMES

There are spots in and around the Andro Village which are mostly engaged for ritual purposes. Again there are streams also in and around the village and they are given the name 'Ahong Turel' and 'Nongmai.

The 'Ahong Turel' originates from a place known as 'Hongtruk' a place at the foot of, 'Nongmaiching' hill. This place 'Hongtruk' is also referred as 'Ahongkei' by Ph. Achou of 'Andro Mamang Leikai'. There is a huge stone at a little height in the hill. This is treated as a sacred place. He is of the opinion that the name of the stream is derived considering its originating place 'Ahongkei' or 'Hongtruk'. This stream runs at the heart of Andro market just at the backside of 'Pureiromba' shrine. Again it passes near the public crematorium in the eastern border of the village. And finally it joins the bigger 'Nongmai' stream which is at the far east of the village. This Nongmai' river flows from north to south at the foot of the eastern hills. A bridge on this stream connects the 'Sanapat Leikai' with the proper Andro Village. The bridge serves as the demarcating point of the stream; the northern side of the bridge is known as 'Ahong Turel' and the southern side of it is known as 'Erang Turel'. Again there are spots like (i) Maibi Fampham, (ii) Sanapat, (iii) Changaithembi, (iv) Lamphel Shoi, (v) Uran Lakpa, (vi) Champra Chingdong, (vii) Leitan Pekpham, (viii) Keko

Pat, (ix) Amamlok, (x) Waktrong, etc. Out of these spots 'Sanapat' and 'Changaithembi' has a clear social and historical background. The remaining others are related with rituals and various other purposes and no proper background is associated with their names. And hence the discussion concentrates on 'Sanapat' and 'Changaithembi'.

I. BACKGROUND OF SANAPAT

It is a lake in Andro which is around three km. away from the proper Andro village. It is in the east of the village. The name 'Sanapat' has a historical background.

King Tabungba (A.D 1359 - 1394) had two sons namely 'Yoirenba' and 'Lairenba' (Punshiba). King Tabungba was killed by a hilltribe along with his close companion in a campaign to collect tribute. So 'Yoirenba' ascended the throne. After a short rule 'Yoirenba' passed away. 'Yoirenba' had no male offspring. So naturally 'Punshiba' had to become King of Manipur.

But "Punshiba' was not immediately available for the throne. Because 'Punshiba' took refuge in the "Moirang' principality which is located in the south western side of the valley. Although it is not clearly mentioned the reason why 'Punshiba' was deported to 'Moirang' in the oral tradition but from the prevailing situation of the then period it seems there was an intense struggle for the throne. Again historically the alliance with 'Moirang' was very much necessary for the capture of the throne in 'Kangla' in Imphal in the event of such power struggle. "Punshiba' was on the search for the throne but he was not available in 'Moirang' because he had already left 'Moirang' from an incident which attempted his life. One day 'Punshiba' participated in a trip in 'Loktak' lake to enjoy the plucking of 'Heikak' (a floating plant bearing thorny fruit). "Punshiba' mistakenly sang a song of Moirang which is strongly objectionable to the community. On hearing the song the 'Moirangs' came out in rage to kill the singer 'Punshiba'. 'Punshiba' on getting prior information escaped from the impending danger and took refuge in a village named 'Kamu' which is around Andro. He narrated the whole event to the King of 'Kamu' and took shelter at the village. He was kept hiding at 'Ningthourot' which later on came to be known as 'Ningthoulok'. This 'Ningthoulok' is near the village 'Torongthel'. At present 'Kamu' village is no longer available. The 'Moirangs' did not stop their search and they gathered the information that 'Punshiba' was hiding in 'Kamu' village. The 'Moirangs' immediately rushed toward 'Kamu' village. Meanwhile 'Kamu' Ningthou (King of Kamu) was aware of the advancing Moirangs. So he immediately shifted 'Punshiba' to Andro and carefully handed over to 'Phanjou Khullakpa'. the chief of Andro. 'Kamu Ningthou' discussed the situation with the seven officials of Andro. And he narrated how 'Punshiba' the prince of 'Kanglei' escaped from the fury of the 'Moirangs' and took shelter at 'Kamu' village. So he explained the vulnerability of his village from the attack of the Moirangs and persuaded the Chief of Andro to take care of the prince. From such an occasion 'Phanjou Khullakpa' the chief of Andro looked after 'Punshiba' like his own son.

The 'Moirangs' continued their hunt for 'Punshiba' even after their failure to capture from 'Kamu' village. They advanced upto Andro Village where they were given a warm welcome and treated with 'Yu' (liquor). While the 'Moirangs' were enjoying 'Yu' lady 'Chakparembi', the wife of 'Phanjou Khullakpa' went to fetch water from 'Kekopat' (a pond) with a 'Sham' (basket) on her back. She carried a 'Pun' (an earthen pitcher) on the 'Sham'. Meanwhile a few 'Moirangs' were in hiding on trees near the community pond, 'Kekopat'. Their intention was to kill Punshiba' if he came out to collect water from the pond. But the opposite happened to their attempt. So the lady on her effort to collect water from the pond she saw the image of the 'Moirang' warriors hiding on the tree in the water. The wishful'Khullakpi' (wife of Khullakpa, the chief) thought of a plan to inform it to her home. To avoid suspicion on her movement she murmured in her mouth that she had forgotten 'Khagok' (a traditional mug made of bamboo or wood) to collect water from the pond without which she could not collect water in the pitcher. So she said herself that she should go back home to bring the 'Khagok' and subsequently left the pond for her home. There at home she informed of the presence of 'Moirang' warriors nearby the .pond in an attempt to ambush someone. The Andro warriors responded quickly and captured 'Moirang Tereba', the commander-in-Chief of the Moirangs. The 'Moirang' warriors who were under the influence of 'Yu' (liquor) came to know that their commander-in-chief had been captured by the Andro warriors. So the 'Moirangs' and the 'Andro warriors fought a pitched battle at 'Kangjeipung' (pologround) of Andro village. In the battle 'Moirang Tereba', commander of the 'Moirangs', was killed by the Andros. From this incident the 'Andros' and the 'Moirangs' had a hostile relationship and one was not allowed to enter other's village. The 'Moirangs' could not enter the shrine of 'Panam Ningthou' for a prayer. Likewise the Andros were not allowed to enter the shrine of 'Thangjing'-the principal deity of the Moirangs. But now they have forgotten the past and have returned to their brotherly relationship.

One day 'Phanjou Khullakpa' accompanied 'Punshiba' in a fishing trip in a lake around Andro. In the course of fishing 'Punshiba' lost his gold ring from his ring finger. From this incident the lake came to be known as 'Sanamang'. But later on it was transformed into 'Sanapat'. Utmost secrecy was maintained while bringing up 'Punshiba'. No name was mentioned while enquiring the prince. Instead the prince was termed as a chicken and enquired that how big was it now, could it craw and had its wings fully grown etc. So only a few persons used this code on enquiring about the prince.

After the death of King 'Yoirenba' there was an interregnum for five years. So there was are intense search for Lairenba (Punshiba) for the throne. After a proverbial long search the palace got the information that 'Punshiba' was taking refuge in Andro. So the palace sent a team of persons to Andro to persuade 'Punshiba' to return to 'Kangla'. The team apprised 'Phanjou Khullakpa' of the difficulties facing in the palace in the vacancy of the throne. His brother 'Yoirenba' is dead without a male heir for the throne. So the throne is vacant for the past five years. He is the younger brother of king 'Yoirenba', and he is a prince. With the above words the team requested 'Phanjou Khullakpa' to hand over the prince so as to enable them to appoint him king of Manipur. 'Phanjou Khullakpa' also readily accepted the request of the team but he also made a request to the team. He had brought up 'Punshiba' as his own son and the young prince also treated 'Khullakpa' as his father. So 'Khullakpa' was unable to release the prince immediately. He made a fervent request to the team to see off the prince on an auspicious day. So on an auspicious day the prince was warmly sent off by the officials of the village along with other elderly persons on the route known as 'Uran Lambi'. The route begins around 'Kharam Leikai' of Andro village. On reaching the hill top 'Punshiba'asked for a rest for awhile. He said, now I had learned that the palace was appointing me king of Manipur. Soon I will become king of Manipur. I have grown up to my adulthood under the care and guidance of my beloved elders of Andro said 'Punshiba'. They were like my father, mother and brothers; he continued. I am heavily indebted of you all. So I request you all to ask me something which I can also offer to you all; he again continued. The elders of Andro were at a fix; they did not know what to say. Looking on the ground they remained pressing their feet on the soil. In such a situation 'Punshiba' realised that what they wanted was land and he granted the boundary of Andro village in the following manner:

1. On the north-western side it touches the 'Eril' river. 2. in the south upto 'Waithou Chingjel' 3. in the east upto 'Thoubal' river. and 4. to the north upto ' Ngairou Chingjel'. In addition to this their land was declared as tax free land. And their lakes could not be autioned.

REFERENCES

1. Oral inlerview with Ph.Achou Andro Mamang Leikai.

II. CHANGAITHEMBI

It is a near plane surface in the 'Nongmaiching' hill . In the ancient past it was a place for serving tiffin to a farmer who went without food. Now the spot is deified to a pilgrimage site and every year the Andros go for a pilgrimage to the spot. The detail background of the spot is discussed. in the introduction of the report.

15

ARTS AND CRAFTS

A. POTTERY IN ANDRO

Pottery ranks one of the oldest craft of the Andros. As found from the literature 'Poirenton Khunthokpa' pottery was known to the Andros before the Christian era. Once Poireiton - the coloniser, in his search for a better place of habitation came across the Andro village. And he saw a bonfire from a distance in the village. He enquired about the fire from a youth. who retorted that the fire was not for puffing rice, for burning straws, for pottery but for cremation. So pottery was well-developed among the Andros and they used fire for burning the pots. As referred by the same literature 'Poirenton' is a contemporary of king Nongda Lairen Pakhangba (A.D 33-A.D. 153). This was a time when there was an intense inter-clan warfare in the region. The authority of the central power was not well established. However, in the later course of history, after many vicissitudes the Ningthouja dynasty could established its hold in the Kingdom. For an effective and suitable administration the chakpas were given their settlement in the peripheral areas adjoining the hills. And the king introduced a social division of production among the chakpa community. As for instance the chakpas of 'Leimaran' and 'Fayeng' were assigned to produce silk cloths from silk-worms. So they were specialised in sericulture. On the other side the Andros .were to supply earthen pots for use in the customary rites and rituals in the capital, Kangla However, with the termination of autocracy in Manipur the tradition also ceased to exist. But it continued its role in the economy of the community and the craft still survives.

In Andro, for pottery, two ingredients are essentially needed. One is 'Leitan' (clay) and the other is 'Leichreng' (coarse soil). And they are located at different locations of the village. For collecting the raw materials certain code is observed and one cannot violate it. Again every year the collection of the raw material, i.e. 'Leitan' and 'Leichreng' begins only after performing their respective rituals on the traditionally appointed days. The ritual named 'Leipka Leiyengba' held on the fifth day of 'Fairen' (January-February) allows the villagers to start collecting 'Leitan'(clay) since the seventh of 'Fairen'. On the other side a ritual named 'Leichreng Leitaba' is held in the month of Mera (SeptemberOctober) which permits the womenfolk to start collecting the 'Leichreng'; the coarse soil.

I. Leipak Leiyengba

As mentioned earlier the clay is available only on a selected place, and the place is locally named as 'Leitan Pekpham'. As discussed earlier the collection of clay is initiated by a ritual named 'L.eipak Leiyengba'. The place do not belong to anyone family but owned by the community. So a community based ritual is performed beginning from the fifth day of 'Fairen' (January- Feb.). At a time when earthen pots were the dominant utensils in the Andro family pottery developed as a household craft. So every family needed a certain amount of clay for their use in a year. With this reality in the background the ceremony 'Leipak Leiyengba' developed as community base ritual. Consequently there arises the need to involve every family in the ceremony. 'Loishang' the village administration enforces the tradition with a heavy hand. Considering the utility and its role in the life of the Andros, the ceremony initiating the collection of 'Laitan' (clay) is conducted with utmost ritual sincerity.

The ritual initiating the collection of clay commences from the fifth day of 'Fairen' (Jan.-Feb.). The ritual is held with the name 'Laipak Leiyengba' in the early hour of morning. This is performed by the 'Pibas' (head of lineage) of 'Phanjoubam', 'Khunnumayum' and 'Ningthoujam' lineage. The ritual is a simple one and it is a prayer to the deity who is supposed to be possessing the open field of around one acre. Subsequent to this ritual, on the next day, the ritual 'Leipak Leithong Hangba' is performed. Since the third day the womenfolk of the village are given permission of collecting the soil.

Ingredients of Leipak Leiyengba

The following items like can sugar, a hen of black colour, 'Yu' (Kalei), Heibi mana (Heibi leaves), a hand of banana of even number (chang thokpa), seven different fruits, seven different flowers, puffed rice (Kabok Khoidum), Kabok Aphaba (puffed rice, loose one), betel nuts and leaves, a small amount of rice, Pukyu (rice bear) and an egg is offered to the deity. This area known as 'Leitan Pekpham' remain unchanged since the olden days. And it continues to do so till these days. This is an open field of around one acre and it has a gentle slope toward the east. A small stream originating from 'Nongmaiching' hill flows in the centre of the ground. In one sense this open field can be termed as an extension of 'Nongmaiching' hill. A small plain is selected in the ground and four small branches are erected at the four corners at a distance of around 15 ft. one from the other. On the eastern side of the secluded place (secluded after erecting the branches) a cane sugar is erected on the ground. Again another cane sugar, around 5 ft. from the previous one in the eastern side, is erected. This easternmost cane sugar is meant for the deity 'Sharoi-Ngaroi'. Now it is the turn to prepare Athenpots - items to be displayed. It is prepared on the western side of the first cane sugar, i.e. inside the secluded place. Three pieces of 'La' (banana leaves) are placed in a row spreading north to south. Just behind this row, i.e. in the western side a bigger banana leaf (Laton) is placed. In this way the Athenpot is prepared by placing cane sugar, fruits, flowers and puffed rice on the three pieces of banana leaves. Cane sugar is shared equally three pieces each. Betel nuts and leaves are also included in the 'Attenpot', 'Kabok Aphaba' is thrown for three times with three handfuls just on the eastern side of the first cane sugar (standing one). Now it is the turn to include egg in the displayed items. A piece of banana leaf is placed in between the long banana leaf and the three pieces where different items are placed. On it a small amount of rice is spread and the egg is rest on it. 'yu' (Kalei) likli - the wine bottle is placed near the Athenpot. Again 'Pukyu' (rice bear) poured on a small bowl is also placed alongside the other items. Thus the required 'Athenpot' is prepared. Lastly a small amount fruits and flowers are also shared for the 'Sharoi- Ngaroi'. But the above items are excluded for it.

After displaying the 'Athenpot' the next part is the sacrifice of the hen. For this the beak and legs of the chicken is washed with water.

A Scene of the ritual 'Leipak Leiyengba.'

Now the throat is slashed with a knife and thus the chicken is sacrificed. Drops of blood are collected on the 'Laton'- the bigger banana leaf. Then the hen is thrown beyond the eastern side of the secluded place. It says that the ritual is performed facing east. The hen is still alive and the direction it faces on its death is to be examined. What follows it is that the blood stained banana leaf is removed from the displayed area and is placed somewhere outside the secluded place.

A small amount of earth is dug out from the place where the stained banana leaf is removed. But at the point of digging the ground the following sentence is uttered - 'Korou Nongthong Hanglabane, Malem Leithong Fatlabane' - which says that 'the sky is opened and the ground is also opened. The next step is to forecast something from the insect available in the ground.

The lump of earth is broken into pieces and carefully examined the embodied insects in the ground. Certain forecast is made based on beliefs by observing the available insects. The belief says; if earthworm is found it will affect the health of children. On the other hand if the insect 'Tingong' is found the coming year will be a plentiful year.

In the concluding part the beak, legs and wings of the hen is cut into small pieces and the same is shared *to* 'three pieces of banana leaves where the Athenpot is displayed.

In the past, as a custom, the sacrificed hen and the rice was cooked at the spot and they used to relish it. But now-a-days a change is observed and the hen is cooked at the house of the 'Piba' who contribute it for this year. The above necessary items included in the ritual is contributed by the three 'Pibas' in yearly rotation. After accomplishing the ritual whatever offered in the ritual is relished by them including the wine, banana, cane sugar and puffed rice, etc.

After accomplishing the ritual the three 'Pibas' immediately returns to the village and submit a report to the 'Khullakpa' that they have successfully performed the ritual 'Leipak Leiyengba'. And further they will make an earnest appeal to the 'Khullakpa' to perform the follow-up ritual 'Leipak Leithong Hangba' the next day. Now it is the turn of 'Khullakpa' and he summons the 'Nambors' where there are four 'Nambors' in the village. He will make known the 'Nambors' that the ritual 'Leipak Leiyengba' is over and further order them to spread the message to the villagers. The 'Nambors' in turn communicate the message to the villagers who are there in one's jurisdiction. They will announce that, *'Leipak Leiyengle'; Leipak Leithong Hangnaba Yum Yumdagi Nupa Amamam Thoklak-U'* - meaning the ritual 'Leipak Leiyengba' is over so a male member from every family should take part in the ritual 'Leipak Leithong Hangba'. The modus operandi of spreading the message is 'Paothang'; that is a 'Nambor' who is in charge of a few Leikais (locals) will select a house which he considers to be the easiest to reach; and to that house he will announce the message. The house in turn will relay the message to his immediate neighbour and the process goes on till the last house. So the 'Nambors' without his physical presence convey the news to his jurisdiction. If any family fails to convey the message to his neighbour he will be fined Rs. *50/-*. In this way the message is spread throughout the length and breadth of the village on the fifth day of 'Fairen' (Jan-Feb). Now the village is ready for the next ritual'Leipak Leithong Hangba' to be held on the next day, i.e. on the sixth day of 'Fairen' .

Leipak Leithong Hangba

In the morning of the sixth day of 'Fairen' the villagers. led by Khullakpa' and the six members of the 'Loishang' assemble at the ritual site where the ritual 'Leipak Leiyengba' was held yesterday. 'Khullakpa', with his six office bearers namely 'Luplakpa', 'Khunjahanba', Khabam Lakpa, 'Yupanba', 'Pakhanglakpa, and 'Nahalakpa' lead the male member of the village in performing 'Leipak Leithong Hangba'. 'Khullakpa' open the ritual with a spade in his hand who makes his first dig. But while doing so he prays to God for an easy and sure access to the 'Leitan' (clay). The inaugural action of the 'Khullakpa' is followed by the villagers and they are in hot pursuit of the clay. They will dig till the soil is appeared. And the ceremony ends when the soil is found out. At the point of departure they will share 'Yu' (liquor) in small amount. This 'Yu' is purchased from the village fund. Someone who is interested may contribute a small amount of 'Yu' on this occasion. In this ceremony also an absentee is punished, not by physical means but by fine. He has to pay his fine in cash. In this age also there is no relax in such punishment. With this simple ceremony the ritual of the sixth day of 'Fairen' ends.

A woman collecting 'Leichreng' (coarse soil) from 'Champra Chingdong.'

The Seventh Day of Fairen

The activity till the sixth day of 'Fairen' is the affair of men. But the seventh day of 'Fairen' is the affair of women. Woman from every family will come out in group and collect the necessary amount of clay for her use. While collecting the clay they use a pointed wooden implement which was prepared by manfolk on the sixth day of 'Fairen', the day of 'Leipak Leithong Hangba', for their use for the purpose. The wooden implement is around 3 ft. in length and the pointed end has two broaden sides. It facilitates in collecting the clay. The implements are around 9,10 in number and prepared considering the women population in the village. It has no fix number. The collection of clay continue till the onset of monsoon. If rain comes it remains practically difficult to collect the soil. With the collection of clay since the seventh day of 'Fairen' a number of new earthen pots of different shapes and sizes are made out of the recently collected raw material. However, as a custom, the raw pots cannot remain unburned till first of 'Shachiphu' (March-April), the Meitei new year day. So all the newly made raw pots are burnt before the first day of 'Shachiphu'. However, one can continue after observing 'Cheiraoba', the Meitei new year.

II. LEICHRENG LEITABA

The ritual performed in connection with the collection of 'Leichreng', the coarse soil, is known as 'Leichreng Leitaba'. It is held in the morning. The ritual is held on the fifth day of 'Mera' (September-October) on a hillock named 'Champra Ch.ingdong'. Generally the ritual is conducted by the three 'Pibas' (head of lineage) of lineages namely 'Khunnumayum', 'Phanjoubam' and 'Ningthoujam'. However, it can be conducted by two 'Pibas' or by a lone 'Piba'. In the case of 'Leipak Leiyengba' the three 'Pibas' are necessarily involved in the ritual. In this ritual also a chicken is necessarily involved. However, in this case, unlike the 'Leipak Leiyengba', the chicken is simply released as scapegoat. The items offered include seven handful of puffed rice, seven different fruits, seven different flowers and rice bear. After accomplishing the ritual by the 'Pibas' then first of all the wife of the 'Pibas' starts collecting the 'Leichreng' (coarse soil). And she collects her necessary amount. Since the next day the women of the village follows in collecting 'Leichreng' till their necessary amount. The collection continues till the last day of 'Enga' (May-June). The hillock is owned By the community.

Preparing mud paste out of 'Leichreng' (coarse soil) and 'Leitan' (clay) for pottery.

Preparing a pot out of mud paste.

Preparation of Mud for Pottery

Before taking up the task of manufacturing pots one needs to prepare the mud paste out of the two ingredients, i.e. 'Leitan' (clay) and 'Leichreng' (coarse soil) with great attention. Because this will decide the fate of the pot when it is burnt in the fire. First of all the clay is broken into pieces with a pestle. Implements needed for the purpose are a few pestles and a dug-out wooden container. It is around 4 ft. in length and is made from a single tree. 'Leichreng'- the coarse soil is first spread on the dug-out. A small amount of water is thrown on it so as to make it wet. This follows the addition of clay but in an equal proportion with the coarse soil. Maintaining the equal proportion in the two ingredients is extremely necessary so as to avoid breakage at the time of burning the pots. The clay is spread above the coarse soil through the length and breadth of the dug-out. The next is the turn of two women who pound it with pestles. Careful pounding is necessary so as to produce a smooth paste. It helps in making a well polished pots; otherwise it produces rough pots with rough surfaces. Now the paste is ready for making pots of different shapes and sizes for different purpose.

The Andro maintain certain code in making pots. Unmarried girls are not allowed to indulge in such activity. Even a married woman who has not crossed six months connot engage in pottery. After six months of her m.arriage she can take part in making pots. The Andros do not practice the wheel pottery and as such is the situation they engage in manual pottery. In making pots the mud paste is manually moulded into a rod and then it is coiled which is locally known as 'Fei Taba'. Certain belief is found embodied in the art of pottery and the same has grown as technique in making pots. The coiled mud rod meet at a point but one end of the rod exceeds the other and this is done deliberately. The belief says that if the two ends of the coiled mud rod meet exactly at a point then death may occur in the family. So in order not to happen such a situation one end of the coiled mud rod is made little longer than the other when they meet at a point.

A small collection of pottery items (raw one).

Implements used in Pottery

Implements used in pottery are very simple. They use a small stick known as 'Tetap', also known as 'Phuyei Cheishu'. They hit the pot at intervals so as to mould into a proper shape. Another tool is a pebble of round shape. It also helps in shaping the pot.

Different Kinds of Pots

1. Yugi Kharung - It is a large jar which is used in preparing 'Yu' (liquor).
2. Walong - It is a medium size jar.
3. Kharung Achouba - It is very large jar which is around 4 ft. in height. In it selective and valuable clothes are stored.
4. 'Pun' (Eshing Pun) - It is used in storing water.

5. Ngankha Chaphu - This is used in cooking.
6. Kegam - It is an earthen plate. It is used as lid of different pots.
7. Koklou - It is a traditional earthen mug. And the same is used in serving 'Waiyu' (rice bear).
8. Tripod - It is used for placing scripts while reciting by a Pandit. Also used for placing flowers and 'Athenpots' in different functions.
9. Koret - It is used in collecting water. It is considered that it adds a flavour to the water.
10. These days earthen lockers for saving coins and stands for lamps are also produced.

These pots are mainly for local consumption. It is not sold in the market. But someone can purchase it from the village. And one can also order to prepare the pots to someone in the village. As a tradition this craft is reserved for women of the village. Men are involved only in the rituals like 'Leipak Leithong Hangba' and 'Leichreng Leitaba'. Aftermath is the task of women. Collecting of 'Leitan' and 'Leichreng', making paste out of the two ingredients are all done by woman. Manufacturing pots and finally burning it in fire is also the task of woman.

B. WOODWORK

Woodwork is still traditional and centered around the production of wooden items like bed, chair, table, side table, cupboard, hand looms, etc. The production is for local consumption and it do not go beyond the village.

C. BAMBOO WORK

Bamboo work produces many items for uses in fishing, harvesting and daily needs. Fishing traps of different types like Kabow Loo, Sora Loo, Taizep, Long-up, etc. and fishing net 'Ell' is prepared by bamboo strips. 'Tungol' - a type of basket which is worn around the waist is also prepared by bamboo strips or chips. Harvesting materials like harvesting net, winnower, etc. are prepared from bamboo. Baskets for stori.ng and measuring paddy and rice like Shangbai, Laitang, Leekhai, Chengchamuk, Meruk, Chak-up, Yendai, etc. are also made from bamboo. Again here the production is for local consumption only and not for sale beyond the village. For its multifarious uses the people maintain certain code in felling bamboo. There are days in a week in which the bamboo cannot be felled. A bamboo cannot be felled on 'Thangja' (Saturday). Every house possess at least a bamboo grove. And every year a small amount of soil is deposited in the bamboo grove which is treated as a routine ritual work.

REFERENCES

1. Oral interview with Ch. Surchandra of Sanapat Leikai, Andro.
2. Oral interview with Sarubam (Ongbi) Dharmomala Devi of Khunou Leikai, Andro.
3. Oral interview with N. Shyam of Andro Mamang Leikai.

16

ECONOMY

The Andro society is a traditional society and so also the economy. As it is the case in other villages in Manipur in the rural areas agriculture is the mainstay of the economy. The villagers are largely depending on traditional tools and implements for farming. They use plough drawn mostly by ox and depends on implements like spade and dao. However, in the recent years they have started using tractors for ploughing. There is no communal ownership of agricultural land, and so individual ownership dominates the scene. As there is no advantage of irrigation so multiple cropping is not popular. They plant a large varieties of paddy including modern high yielding varieties. The product of paddy is little above subsistence level, and so they export paddy to other areas of Manipur. Gardening is popular in Andro and they plant a variety of vegetables mostly for their consumption. Gardening for export is not very successful due to many reasons. For their village consumption they plant cabbage, onion, garlic, mustard, banana plants, peas, chowhawai, hawai ashangbi, koli hawai, gourd, sebot, yendem, chilli" ginger, .hawai amubi, turmeric, potato etc. Cane sugar is also planted. Silk worm is reared. Fruits like lemon, mango, guava etc. are also planted. 'Yongchak' is the only vegetable which is exported outside Andro serving as a seasonal income to many families of Andro. Thatch garden is owned communally in the distant areas of the village. However, cotton plantation is not so popular in Andro. In the past the required cotton in bulk was got from the hills.

A display of some of the fishing implements.

Another side income of Andro is 'Yu' (liquor) which can be counted as by-product of agriculture. Formerly 'Yu' of different kinds both strong and soft, was prepared mainly for religious uses and home consumption. But now it is a source of income and this 'Yu' is exported to other areas of Manipur which is popular for its taste and effectiveness. In this areas also the technique of production is still traditional and there is need for modernisation. If necessary steps are taken to modernise the production with a view to export it beyond Manipur or beyond India it will be a great source of income in future. Efforts are being made by the villagers themselves to modernise their agriculture by introducing winter variety of paddy. However it fail because of lack of irrigation. However, an ambitious plan is the plantation of mulberry plants in the hilly areas of Andro. The plantation has been introduced in view of the sericulture project - a joint project of the Govt. of Manipur and Japan. When materialised it will help in transforming the economy of Andro in particular and Manipur in general. Another ensuing crop is 'Jatropha' which is locally known as 'Awa Kege'.

'Jatropha' is grown in wild in Andro without no use. When the production is introduced in this village also this will be an addition to their economy. Again efforts are being made to introduce irrigation to the farms of Andro under a scheme known as 'Thoubal Project'. When the scheme is materialised in a year or so the irrigation in their farms will help in developing their economy. This will largely help in transforming their outlook. attitude and their social life which ultimately lead to dispelling their isolationist view. The largely' domesticated animals of the Andros are cattle. pig. dog. chicken and cat, etc. Buffalo and goat is not popular in Andro, Goat is not domesticated and they avoid their meat also. They also rear bee for honey. But all these are for home consumption only not for sale to other areas. Pottery is popular in Andro however. this is also for home consumption only.

Wood works and bamboo works are still traditional. From wood they produce table, chair. bed, cupboard, loom, door, windows, side table, etc. From bamboo they produce a number of items for use in fishing, harvesting and storing and measuring pots of paddy, etc. Fishing traps of different types like Kabow 100. Sora 100, Taizep, longup, etc. and 'Ell' the fishing net; Tungol the fish container are prepared by bamboo chips. Harvesting materials like harvesting mat, winnowers, etc. and baskets of different purpose ranging from measuring to storing like Shangbai, Laitang, Leekhai, Chengchamuk, Meeruk, Chak-up, Yendai, etc. are also made from bamboo chips. 'Tareng'- spinning wheel is also prepared by cane and bamboo chips. Again from bamboo chips they also prepare 'Long-up' for catching 'Kaojeng' (grasshopper). Again the production in this area is also for local consumption only and not for sale beyond the village. Last but not the least 'is the earning from services both from state and central services.

Many of them are employed in para-military and military of India which serves as remittance from beyond the state.

REFERENCE

1. Oral interview with Ch. Thambal of Andro Awang Leikai.

17

CHAKPA VOCABULARY

A. WORDS

	(Chakpa)	(Manipuri)	(English)
1.	Anganga	Ema	Mother
2.	Onwa	Epa	Father
3.	Okshuwako	Epen	Grandmother
4.	Ashangngako	Emahan	
5.	Oksi	Epu	Grandfather
6.	Awang	Khura, Eton	Uncle
7.	Mamak	Endon	Aunty
8.	Aapao	Eyamba	Elder brother
9.	Miyou	Eteima	Sister-in-law
10.	Aapi	Ene (Epagi Mache amadi Machan)	Fathers' sisters
11.	Aaneng	Epai, Ebai	Brother-in-law
12.	Nganingsha	Eshen	Brother-in-law
13.	Chan	Echan	Youger sister
14.	Aamang	Mamma	Mother's brothers

(Chakpa)	(Manipuri)	(English)
15. Aani	Ene (Mammana Louba Ene, Epagi Mache Machansing)	Father's sisters
16. Aaning	Enempok	Mother-in-law
17. Aaku	Eku	Father-in-law
18. Uta	Etao	Friend
19. Ngasharei	Echasha	My sons
20. Ngannarei	Enaosha	My younger brothers
21. Tu	Hawai	Dal
22. Ashamunga		
23. Shayaji	Oja	Teacher
24. Shuwang	Ningthou	King
25. Olon	Hou	
26. Kichi	Meitei, the majority	(Meitei community)
27. Shok	Shan	Cattle
28. Ke	Eroi	Buffalo
29. Wak	Ok	Pig
30. Kilangtong	Shagol	Horse
31. Ki	Hui	Dog
32. Kemon	Houdong	Cat
33. U	Yen	Chicken
.34. Urailong	Yen Laba	Cock
35. Ununang	Yenpi	Hen
36. Aam	Phou	Paddy
37. Huchat	Cheng	Rice

(Chakpa)	(Manipuri)	(English)
38. Khachikpom	Atingba	Rice Bear
39. Kan	E (Yum Kupnaba)	Thatch
40. Liyou	Labuk	Paddy field
41. Chamit	Numit	Sun
42. Sata	Tha	Moon
43. Chum pang	Thawanmichak	Star
44. Hiktok	Leichil	Cloud
45. Kem	Chum	Lizard
46. Ka	Leipak	Soil
47. Harang	Nongthou (Atiya)	Sky.
48. Karamsiyo	Phajeiye	It is beautiful
49. Malthang	Mamangthong	Front Door
50. Sempreng	Maningthong	Back Door
51. Srep	Saigang (Yennakha)	The side of house
52. Solong	Sumang	Courtyard
53. Chamitpukto	Numit Thorakle	The sun rises
54. Aaiyeptafo	Hougatlo	Get up
B. SENTENCES		
55. Wanfale	Mei Hougatio	Lit up fir
56. Kohongnachu	Chak Thonglage	Let me cook rice
57. Huchatlahare	Cheng Puraklo	Bring rice
58. Mekanhon-gchungai	Kari Enshang	What curry do you want to cook? Thonggeba
59. Tangngah-ongchu	Nga Thongngo	Cook the fish.

(Chakpa)	(Manipuri)	(English)
60. Wak Hongchu	Ok Thongngo	Cook the hog.
61. U Hongchu	Yen Thongngo	Cook the Chicken.
62. Kamun Hongmungngo	Hanggam Thongngo	Cook the mustard.
63. Kosharachu	Chak Charshi	Let us eat rice.
64. Sarachu	Charo	Eat the rice or anything.
65. Utuk khuhongnung	Khunu Thongngo	Cook the pigeon.
66. Ushihong-nungngo	Laphu Thongngo	Cook the banana stem.
67. Tu Hongmengngo	Hawai Thongngo	Cook the dal.
68. Miyoushang chungai	Katai Chatlugeba	Where are you going?
69. Megakachan-nungnge	Kari Thabak Touriba	What are you doing?
70. Un Nungngo	Lak-ebara	Are you visting us?
71. Un Nunge	Lak-e	Yes, I am visiting.
72. Mekachage Nalinungngo	Kari Thabakki Lakpano	For what purpose are you visiting us.
73. Koshanungngo	Chak Chadri	I have not taken food.
74. Koshakata	Chak Chare	I have taken food.
75. Me Uchu Lahare	Eshing Purak-O Thakke	Bring Water, let me drink it.
76. To Uchu Lahare	Yu Purak-U Thakke	Bring liquor, let me drink it.

(Chakpa)	(Manipuri)	(English)
77. Kan Tamangchu	E Phanluge	Let me go to harvest thatch.
78. Uchu	Thakke	Let me drink.
79. Tangnga tamangchu	Nga Thiruge	Let me search fish.
80. Chumlar-angchu	Thum Louruge	Let me collect salt.
81. Lisharak	Chellak-O	Run toward me.
82. Ketamangchu	E-roithiruge	Let me go to search buffalo.
83. Shoktam-	Shan Thiruge	Let me go to to search angchu cattle.
84. Aamlang-ngachu	Phou Holluke	Let me go to collect paddy.
85. Riyouwak Kinsiham-angchu	Louda Loo Thummuge	Let me go to lay fish trap in the paddy field.
86. Phunchu	Phi Purak-u	Bring cloth.
87. Yeke	En-ge (Fi)	Let me wear cloth.
88. Sorong Kangte	Phak Thao	Offer a seat on mat.
89. Tehongkangte	Phan Thao	Offer a seat on the wooden plank.
90. Sengchun-telahare	Hidak Halle	The pipe is ready for smoking.
91. Liyouwakme-tamangchu	Louda Eshing Yeng-ge	Let me go to to check water in the paddy field.

(Chakpa)	(Manipuri)	(English)
92. Wanchangte	Mei Chakte	The fire is not live.
93. Wanmutkado	Mei Hapmo	Put the fire on the pipe.
94. Singgong krato	Hidakphu Lou-o	Take the smoking pipe.
95. Mekhwakchu	Erujage	Let me take bath.
96. Mehang-ngakhongnachu	Turelda Erujaruge	Let me take bath in the river.
97. Ngayeplachu	Ei Tumning-nge	I am sleepy.
98. Ukak-o	Thakning-nge	I want to drink.
99. Langte	Lourucho	Go and collect.
100. Sarachu	Chatlasi	Let us go.

REFERENCE

Prepared in consultation with Heikrujam Angousana of Andro Khunou Leikai.

18

CONCLUSION

The Andros (Chakpa), a component of the bigger Meitei community, constitute one of the oldest people of this region. At what time and from which direction did the Andros (chakpa) came is still a matter of controversy, although it is mentioned in the literature 'Kangbaron' that the 'Chakpas' first appeared during the reign of 'King Moria Phambalcha' who ruled in Manipur before the Christian era. Their arrival in 'Yoishangkai' - an office in the palace, the subsequent departure from 'Nongmeibung' and finally settlement at the 'Nongmaiching' hill is clearly mentioned in the literature 'Pakhangba Khundoklol'. However, this differs with the oral tradition of the village which says that the Andro once settled at different places of Imphal viz. at Kakwa, Wangkhei and Pureiromba, etc. However, they also agree that a group of Andros settled at 'Nongmaiching' in the ancient past. And at a certain point of time they came down from the hill and settled at the foot of the hill for the first time at the place named 'Khuman' which later on came to be known as 'Khuman leikai'. At one point of time 'Nongmaiching' was the home many tribes viz., Angom, Shelloi langmai, Andros. Tangkhul etc. and there were villages like Haokam, Chingshang, Ngangcheng, Khulpham, Thanga Youkhan, etc. The proximity of Andros with the 'Angom' clan and their intimacy in cultural relationship may be one reason why

'Pureiromba' and 'Chingshomba' have been included in the pantheon of their sylvan deities. Their long settlement on 'Nongmaiching' hill developed a close intimacy with this hill which is reflected in the ritual 'Chupsa Moithemba' where the mountain and its nine ranges are symbolically represented by a heap of rice and nine rows of rice put on plantain leaves.

There are many areas which are similar with that of the Meiteis in the midst of many dissimilarities in many other areas. The architecture of the traditional four or five roomed house and beliefs embodied in the architecture is almost the same with that of the Meiteis. Again in the aspect of terms of address in the kinship and outside the matter remains the same with the Meiteis. The Andros also worship the same household deities viz. Sanamahi, Leimaren, Emoinu, etc. at their designated secluded places. The difference in the items offered in these deities may have appeared only after the adoption of Hinduism by the Meiteis. There are references in the archaic literatures about the use of 'Yu' and meat in the marriage and death ceremonies among the Meities in the past. A vivid account of this is available from the literature 'Panthoibi Khongkul'. In the aspect of beliefs and practices many of are similar with that of the Meiteis, however, some minor differences also figured in this area also. Wits test is almost similar with the Meiteis, although the abundance of literary taste is a matter which one has to praise liberally considering the environment which one hardly expects. In the case of marriage the engagement form of age dominated the scene in both the communities which was time consuming and uneconomical. For the Andros an elderly person (male) is the link man of the two families till the stage when the two families ceremonially agrees for the marriage of their children. Again this is not the case among the Meiteis where it is an elderly woman who serves as the link man of the two families. In this case also she retires at the stage when the two families formally committed for the marriage at a ceremony where members of the families in their neighbourhood also present. In both the communities the marriage rule was very harsh and and engagement was the only socially sanctioned kind of marriage. The one who breached these customary law was severely punished in many forms. However, in these day things are changed, and the people in both the communities are adopting shorter and easier form of marriage 'Chelhong'- the elopement.

The process of disposal of death is one area where the distinct identity of the Andros emerges. The shooting of 'Lai' by the death person using an arrow and catapult, paintings on the coffin, again the shooting the funeral pyre by a catapult before it is burnt are the practices where the Meiteis do not have any idea. The institution of 'Maksha' and 'Ningol Matung Enba' are unique in its character. They are the two persons who will cremate the person (death) where it is the community who are engaged in the cremation in other communities including the Meiteis. The act of marching with burning rice including dry fishes on a 'Kambi' (earthen plate) in the nights beginning from the day of cremation till the day of death ceremony is not found practised by the Meities. Again the belief associated with the practice is totally void among the Meities. The use of 'Miren Polang', (a basket like structure made of bamboo chips) a structural representation of the deceased person, is another addition to the already mentioned differences. However, the treatment on the existence of soul remain similar in both the communities. The belief says that the soul do not leave the body and the family immediately after death. It stays somewhere in and around the house or in the village. So the marching with burning rice and the use of 'Miren Polang' is a clear testimony to this belief.

It is not certain that there were such institutions like 'Pujarishang' and 'Arangbashang' in Meitei society at one time. But for the 'Andros' the non-existence of professional 'Pujari' and 'Arangpham' in their society may be one reason for the emergence of such socio-cultural institutions. The introduction of modern education and the subsequent services in the state and other areas is a continuous blows to such socio-cultural institutions. The Andros are not behind the Meiteis as far as the ritual and festivals are concerned considering its number and variety. Out of the twelve months eight month are engaged either in one ritual or a festival. And generally the rituals and festivals are very time consuming and many of the rituals or festivals are performed throughout the day. There are rituals which are identical in name with that of the Meiteis but differences crop up as regard the ingredients of offering as well as in timing. As an instance 'Kurak Lamtaiba' is common to both the communities, however, there is a difference in the timing of the ritual. For the Meiteis it is held in the beginning of rainy season whereas the Andros perform the ritual at the fag end of rainy season where preparations are made for harvesting. However, in both the communities the motive behind the prayer remain the same, a prayer for a good harvest.

Among the various rituals and festivals one very interesting event is 'Laisha Tanba'. This term 'Laisha Tanba' is found mentioned in the literature 'Panthoipi Khongkul'. It is an event of ritual hunting where the hunted game is offered to the concerned deity. This was once practised by the Meiteis but it has been abandoned at a certain point of time in which no one has mentioned of it. Even it has no image in the vocabulary of Meiteilon (Meitei language). But the Andros by its very sense of preserving things they have continued this ritual hunting for thousands of years. Thanks to their sense of preserving things. Although it is a sport of hunting animals for offering to deity but it speaks much about their martial character. Evidently this is a dangerous game where someone may face death or severe injury from the act of ferocious hunting. Although 'Khunthong Latpa', 'Cheiraoba', 'Lang ban Chakhangba' and 'Ningol Chakouba' are common to both the communities there are differences in the procedure of the rituals and as well as in timing, place of offering and ingredients offered, etc. However, the ritual 'Maibi Chaklon Katpa' and 'Lam Haiba' are purely a matter of the Andros. No such rituals are found among the Meiteis. 'Maibi Chaklon Katpa' is directly related with their main festivals viz. 'Panam Haraoba' and 'Pureiromba Haraoba'. It is a substitute of their main festivals. As the shrine of 'Panam' is replaced by concrete structure which may last many decades there is the chance of holding this 'Maibi Chaklon Katpa' for many decades without any break.

Panam and Pureiromba rank to the sylvan deities of Manipur, however, due emphasis is given to 'Panam' particularly during the festival. No outsider is allowed to enter or stay in the village during Haraoba festival. Whatever importance may be given to this deity but what is really performed in the Haraoba festival is nothing but a fertility ritual - a prayer for good health, harvest and a large population. Interestingly this sense of fertility is found scattered in various actions and activities and moments of life. The counting of 'Chang-Shi-Chang' while purchasing a hand of banana, a Yangkok (winnower), a mat and while preparing Athenpots, etc. are the embodiment of fertility cult. It is life which is remembered while counting and purchasing things. They do not like to purchase a thing which may destroy their life. Even at the time of earthquake they shout 'Chak-Nga' (rice and fish) which expresses the desire of wealth and abundance of food. But why such a deep sense of fertility among the people of this region? Such a sense night have been born because of numerous enemies of mankind ranging from animals, insects, diseases and many dangerous natural calamities. In short for every step taken mankind had to face one or many enemies which threatens their lives.

Moreover, mankind had a little knowledge of his environment and diseases. So there was an insurmountable threat to their lives which may simply swept away a tribe or a village in a given unfavourable situation. In the given circumstance of smallness of population there is always a tendency to increase the population by any available means. Such a tendency has eventually transformed into a sense of fertility in their posterity. Such a sense of such a practice has its continuity till date when mankind is relatively free from the above mentioned dangers and difficulties.

The Loishang (the village authority) - the centre of temporal and spiritual power at one time during the monarchy; its power has been curtailed significantly since the advent of democracy in Manipur. Parts of its judiciary power has been transferred to modern law court. The introduction of modern economy and education on one hand and the influence of great religions like Hinduism and Christianity on the other is certainly a dual attack to their tradition and custom. Social institutions like 'Shiglup', 'Maksha' and 'Ningol Matung Enba', 'Arangba and Pujari Loishang', 'Pana' organisation, etc. certainly help in cementing their community to a monolithic society. But a transformation in their economy is visible in the near future with different schemes relating to irrigation, introduction of mulberry plantation, Jatropha and various winter resistant crops on the plan which subsequently will increase their mobility in goods and services. The birth of a new middle class is in the offing who are relatively economical in the use of time and money. Whether such a new class will comply the time consuming and uneconomical rituals and festivals or simply act against the traditional normal is a big question to the village authority. Certainly a psychological preparation is necessary to transform this socio-cultural institutions in view of the impending transformation correspondingly in the economic and educational areas.

INDEX